WHO WROTE THE
BIBLE CODE?

WHO WROTE THE
BIBLE CODE?

A PHYSICIST PROBES THE CURRENT CONTROVERSY

RANDALL INGERMANSON, PH.D.

WATERBROOK
PRESS

WHO WROTE THE BIBLE CODE?
PUBLISHED BY WATERBROOK PRESS
5446 North Academy Boulevard, Suite 200
Colorado Springs, Colorado 80918
A division of Random House, Inc.

ISBN 1-57856-225-2

Library of Congress Cataloging-in-Publication Data
    Who wrote the Bible code? : a physicist probes the current controversy / Randall
Ingermanson. — 1st ed.
        p.   cm.
    Includes bibliographical references.
    ISBN 1-57856-225-2 (pbk.)
    1. Ciphers in the Bible.   I. Title.
    BS534.I26   1999
    221.6'8—dc21   99-21780
                                                                        CIP

Printed in the United States of America
1999—First Edition

10 9 8 7 6 5 4 3 2 1

To Eunice and our girls:
Carolyn, Gracie, Amy

———————

CONTENTS

Tables and Figures

ACKNOWLEDGMENTS

I thank:

- Yoni Adonyi, Barney Kasdan, and Hadara Hyman—for overseeing the various stages of my study of Hebrew

- John Thomley, Jeanie Sullivan, and Shira Wiseman—colaborers in my advanced Hebrew class

- Jeff Hilton, Michael Hyman, and Jay and Esther Hill—for technical discussions

- Don Williams; Jay Hoehn; David, Becca, Sarah, and Daniel Poage; Mark and Gail Lundgren; Jeff and Kristine Magee; and Tony and Kym Halstead—my friends at the Coast Vineyard who rarely failed to ask how the book was coming and never tried to escape when I told them

- Gary and Sandy Becker, Ron and Kahanah Farnsworth, Jeanette Conacher, John Sabin, and Richard Andrades—my friends at Kehilat Ariel who believed this book would find a publisher when I wasn't so sure

- Steve Moore and Donna Axelrod—for teaching me to write

- Ron Haynes—my agent, who went to his reward shortly before I began this project

- Elaine Wright Colvin—director of Writers Information Network, for good advice and a tough critique

- Jan Collins—for putting me straight on alphabets, phonetic and otherwise

- Mike Carroll—artist extraordinaire, writing buddy, and general lunatic

- Claire West—terrific writer and the world's most perceptive critic, who browbeat me until those first three chapters worked

- John DeSimone—my writing buddy since the Stone Age, who kept me writing when the only sane thing to do was quit

- John Olson—my writing buddy, practically a brother, who has more ideas in a week than I get in a year and who believes in me far more than I do

- Harold Gans and Barry Simon—for several technical discussions by e-mail

- Dave and Heather Kopp—for vaulting me past the slush pile

- Erin Healy and Thomas Womack—two terrific editors who discovered me and turned my manuscript into a book

- Eunice—for being mine

READING BETWEEN THE LINES

Reading between the lines can get you in trouble.

I discovered this when my wife, Eunice, confronted me about a nude model named Denice.

"I found this note on your desk," Eunice said. "Who's Denice? Where did you meet this nude model?"

Mystified, I grabbed the sheet of paper and stared at it. My own hand scribbling — no doubt about it.

I should mention that I'm a computational physicist, and I've spent the last year writing a large software system to analyze networks of interacting devices.

I jabbed my finger at one of the words. "That letter is a v, not an n," I said. "The word is 'Device,' not 'Denice.'"

Eunice's mouth twitched, a sure sign that she was trying not to smile. "Okay…maybe. But what about the nude model?"

"This word is 'node,' not 'nude,'" I said. "These notes are all about networks — devices, nodes, models. Besides, Denise is spelled with an s, not a c."

At that point Eunice broke out laughing and quit teasing me about my bad handwriting.

Which brings me to the topic of this book.

In the last few years, a number of good souls have concluded that God writes between the lines — that He has hidden a "Bible code" in the text of the Hebrew Bible for us to find.

At first glance this seems an absurd notion. Why would God do such a thing? What's the point?

A second glance only compounds the absurdities. The methods used by some of these folks look naive in the extreme. Patterns? What patterns? You can see any pattern or message you want if you look long enough. For example, "nude model Denice." Unlike my wife, though, these people aren't kidding.

But several prominent mathematicians have taken a third glance and decided that the matter isn't so simple. True, some of the "evidence" for the Bible code looks so flimsy that it's hardly worth taking time to demolish. And yet...

And yet scientists have claimed, after obtaining startling results from a set of computer experiments, that there can be no natural explanation for them. Could God be behind this?

It's an excellent question, and it will occupy us for the rest of these pages.

IS THE BIBLE CODE AUTHENTIC?

My purpose in *Who Wrote the Bible Code?* is to answer two questions: Does the Bible really hide some intentionally encoded patterns? And, if so, who wrote them? At present, people have suggested three possible answers to these questions:

1. The Bible code is without validity or substance, and at worst it is a hoax; therefore nobody wrote it.

2. God wrote the Bible code.

3. Space aliens wrote the Bible code.

Does it really matter? you may be asking. Isn't this just goofiness?

Yes, it really matters, despite the fact that some of the Bible-code people have gotten rather carried away. It truly matters for two reasons:

1. The Bible code is being touted in some quarters as a "proof of God's existence" —the ultimate evangelistic tool.

2. Others are using the Bible code as a high-tech Ouija board, finding predictions of imminent disaster or apocalypse.

Both approaches are wrongheaded and dangerous, I believe.

Let's take the prediction aspect first. Everyone agrees that if the Bible code is real, then it must have been put there by superhuman intelligence. This implies that the message of the Bible should be taken seriously. But the Bible expressly forbids divination (Leviticus 19:26; Deuteronomy 18:10,14)! On the other hand, if the Bible code is not real or authentic, then its predictions are worthless. In either case, using the Bible code for fortunetelling doesn't make sense!

One misguided Bible-coder found this out the hard way when he predicted the Rapture on May 31, 1998. His apology after that date was admirable for its honesty but painful to read. I can't believe that God approves of this kind of prophetic high jinks.

But what about the evangelists using the Bible code to bring people to God? What's wrong with that?

What's wrong is that the evidence for the Bible code is weaker than these people claim. Much weaker.

Suppose the Bible code is a hoax. Then people are being deceived into believing in God. That's wrong! If you think that the end justifies the means, please think again. Eventually the hoax will be exposed. Then what will happen to all those converts?

On the other hand, suppose the Bible code is real. Suppose a pattern underlies the text of the Bible. Suppose we can find this pattern and prove that it was put there intentionally. Suppose this pattern encodes knowledge far beyond the abilities of any ancient peoples. Proof of the pattern would be the most remarkable discovery in a century of remarkable discoveries. If the proof is there, let's find it! But we need strong proof, not the flimsy evidence we've seen so far.

We're cheating ourselves if we accept the half-convincing evidence that's been given to date. We're allowing the whole issue to be muddied with a number of naive and weird ideas, giving God and the Bible a bad name.

Understand that I'm not afraid of weird ideas. I'm a physicist. We're the people who believe that space and time are curved, that everything from electrons to eggplants to elephants is fuzzy probability waves, that the theory of the universe may be best expressed by one-dimensional superstrings that live in ten dimensions and curl up into four. We physicists unlocked the secrets of semiconductors and superconductors, of black holes and wormholes, of lasers and masers and quasars.

The universe is a weird place and we might as well get used to it.

But the ultimate test of any theory is the experimental evidence. Physicists don't buy into strange theories simply for the sake of weirdness. We buy into them only when we can find indisputable evidence that they're correct.

So what about the Bible code? Weird but unproved, right?

Yes, so far. I believe that we can settle the authenticity question using a completely new test that I've developed. Actually it's not one test, but four. They're simple but subtle. Simple enough that I can explain them to my nonmathematical friends in an evening or so. Subtle enough that it'll take a book this size to work out all the details.

Once we've decided whether the Bible code is real or not, we can more easily answer the question of authorship. I'll present answers to both questions in this book.

That's a fairly tall order for one thin book. Here's what we have to do to succeed:

- We need to understand what people have already said about the Bible code.
- We need to develop an arsenal of objective tests to determine the Bible code's authenticity.
- We need to write some software to do the hard work of running those tests.
- We need to apply the tests to the Bible, using the software.
- Based on the test results, we need to evaluate whether the Bible code is real, then decide how to respond to what we discover.

We're going to do all five of these in this book. I hope you like a good mystery, because that's what we have here. If you're the type who reads the last page of mysteries first to see whodunit, then I'll tell you right now that the answer is in chapter 13 of this book. But you wouldn't peek, would you? The fun is in figuring out the puzzle.

I invite you to play the role of Dr. Watson in this mystery. There is an answer, and we're going to find it. I guarantee the search will be more rewarding than trying to figure out the identity of "nude model Denice."

WHAT TOOLS DO WE NEED?

You may be wondering what skills we'll need to solve this mystery. Do we need to know Hebrew? Do we need a Ph.D. in rocket surgery? Do we need a year's time on a Cray supercomputer?

No, no, and no.

I do happen to read Hebrew, but on this project we're going to make the computer do all the reading. I also have a Ph.D. in physics from the University of California at Berkeley, but we won't need any mind-bending mathematics for this puzzle. Nor will a Cray supercomputer be necessary — the calculations will run on a home computer in a few hours. I'm posting my software for free on the Internet so you can check the results for yourself. If you have Java on your computer, you can run this software. (See "A Final Note" at the back of this book for the details.)

A few comments on our methods are in order.

First, we're going to run a careful, sober experiment here. The Bible code has been wildly sensationalized. Many people have formed an opinion based more on emotion than evidence. This seems to be as true of the skeptics as of the believers.

Second, I want to clarify that I don't have a strong emotional investment in either side of the argument. I'm interested in finding out the truth, and I'm sure you are too. (By the way, most of this book — including the parts describing the tests we must develop to determine the Bible code's authenticity — was written *before* the tests were actually run.) If we find that the Bible code is real, then that will be extraordinary, exciting news. If we discover that it's not real, then it'll be a great relief to settle the issue once and for all, so we can get on with our lives. Either way, truth will win. Isn't that the important thing?

OUR PLAN

Here's the plan for our investigation.

In the next three chapters we're going to do our homework on the Bible code. We need to find out what's been done already so we don't waste time following paths that have already been walked. We also need to critically evaluate what others have said. Do these people make sense? Or are there holes in their logic or approach? Are they blowing smoke?

Once we understand the Bible code, we'll need to think a bit about the relationship between language and math. It turns out that languages have mathematical properties that we can measure. Most people already have some intuition about these, but we'll define them precisely. If you have a technical background, you'll probably want to see the equations. I'm going to hide those in Appendices A through D (which are located on my Web site—see "A Final Note" at the back of this book). The math isn't really very hard, but neither is it necessary in order to understand the principles. If you don't care for math, don't read the appendices.

With this background in linguistic measurements, we'll be ready to devise a set of four different tests for the Bible code. Any one of these tests would be enough, but it will be reassuring to find that all four give the same results. We'll spend several chapters developing our tests and checking that they work on "control texts" — nonbiblical texts that certainly don't carry any secret coded messages from God. We'll first apply our methods to a sequence of fifty thousand random numbers, then to Dr. Seuss's children's book *The Cat in the Hat,* then to an English translation of Genesis, and finally to a Hebrew translation of Tolstoy's epic novel *War and Peace.* Only this last text is written in Hebrew, but that won't cause us any problems. Our methods will work with any language that uses a phonetic alphabet.

Once we have an arsenal of tests, we can work on the Bible code. It'll take only two chapters to solve the main mystery. After that, we'll wrap up all the loose ends.

Are you ready? Let's get started.

2

ALPHABET SOUP

My daughter Amy's birth was prophesied thousands of years ago, and I can prove it.

Suspicious?

Good. There is such a thing as healthy skepticism.

Here's the "proof" that Amy is a prophetic child. The alphabet is thousands of years old, and Amy is only five. Yet her name is embedded in the text of the alphabet at an interval of twelve letters. You can see it plainly by writing the alphabet in rows of twelve. For easy identification, I've capitalized the letters of her name:

```
A   b   c   d   e   f   g   h   i   j   k   l
M   n   o   p   q   r   s   t   u   v   w   x
Y   z
```

I've written the alphabet in rows of twelve letters solely for convenience, so that Amy's name runs down the first column. This was not essential though. Had I used rows of a different length, say eleven letters, her name would still be there, but it would run down a diagonal. It's simply easier to spot when the length of the rows is the same as the interval between letters.

We've found what people call an Equidistant Letter Sequence, usually abbreviated ELS. Like any ELS, this one can be uniquely identified by three numbers: 1, 12, and 3. The number 1 is the letter position where the ELS begins within the text (the alphabet, in this case), 12 is the interval between letters, and 3 is the length of the ELS.

Now note this amazing fact. Amy was born on January 12, that is, 1/12. Furthermore, she is the third daughter in my family. There you have it: 1, 12, and 3 — precisely the numbers that uniquely define her ELS!

What are the odds of such an amazing coincidence? Doesn't this prove that Amy's birth was prophesied long ago?

Your intuition should be shrieking right now: This is absurd! There must be a simple explanation.

You may think that I've lied to you. Perhaps I don't really have a daughter named Amy. Or maybe she wasn't really born on January 12. And is she really my third child?

I assure you I haven't lied. And yet I don't believe there's anything more here than random coincidence. I happened to notice that "Amy" was an ELS in the alphabet while testing some of the software I wrote for this book. Then it occurred to me that I could assign "meaning" to the numbers 1, 12, and 3 by determining how each applied to Amy. Had she been born on December 1, I'd have reassigned the "meaning" of 12 and 1 to fit those facts.

This little exercise provides a warning for us. Life is full of coincidences, but coincidences don't always mean something.

Sometimes, however, they do. For proof of that, turn to Psalm 46 in the *King James Version* of the Bible. Count down to the forty-sixth word in this chapter. You'll find the word "shake." Count backward forty-six words from the end of the chapter, ignoring the "Selah." You'll find "spear." This passage was translated in 1610, the year William Shakespeare turned forty-six!

Are all these forty-sixes a meaningless coincidence? Probably not. The translators appear to have taken a little liberty with the text to honor the Bard.

We conclude that a coincidence may or may not be meaningful. In this book we're going to define very carefully how to tell when a coincidence is meaningful and when it isn't.

Why do we have to go to such trouble?

Because that's what the Bible code is — a set of coincidences involving one or more ELSs, coincidences that may or may not be meaningful.

But before we get into our study of coincidences, let's discuss what has already been written about the Bible code, beginning with an overview in this chapter. Chapter 3 will explain the details of one very famous experiment. In chapter 4, we'll kick the tires on the experiment a bit, probing for weak spots.

We're going to be very thorough in these three chapters, very nitpicky. By the time we've finished thrashing things through, we'll be ready to do some real research.

A BRIEF HISTORY OF THE BIBLE CODE

People have been finding amusing patterns like my "Amy" ELS in the text of the Hebrew Bible for centuries. Until the 1980s, however, they remained just that — amusing patterns that could be dismissed as accidents. Coincidences.

Then Eliyahu Rips became interested in the Bible code. Rips, a professor at Hebrew University in Jerusalem, has an international reputation in a branch of mathematics known as "group theory." When he immigrated to Israel from his native Lithuania, he was an atheist. But in Jerusalem he began to hear about strange mathematical patterns in the Torah, the first five books of the Bible. Ultimately he joined the thriving Orthodox Jewish community. Since then he's been a major force in introducing the Bible code to other mathematicians and physicists.

In the mid-1980s, Rips was joined by Doron Witztum, a young Israeli graduate student who had left physics to "study Torah." Witztum is widely described as "the leading Bible-code researcher in the world." Between them, Rips and Witztum put the analysis of the code on a much sounder mathematical footing. They not only looked for coincidences, but they also tried to compute the probabilities of those coincidences.

Together with Yoav Rosenberg, a computer scientist from the Jerusalem College of Technology, Rips and Witztum wrote an article in the British *Journal of the Royal Statistical Society* on the patterns they had discovered. They followed this up with a second article, which appeared in August 1994 in an American journal, *Statistical Science*.

This second article underwent intense scrutiny by several referees before it was accepted for publication. It was carefully prepared and has been widely studied by both believers and skeptics. In essence, the paper presents evidence that the author of Genesis intentionally encoded information about future events into the text.

Several prominent mathematicians have gone on record as saying that this is serious research that deserves a careful look. These men are not endorsing the interpretation, of course. They're simply saying that the Bible code has not been disproved, but neither has it been proved.

A few American and Israeli scientists have gone further though. They've seen the evidence, and they're convinced.

On the other hand, quite a few scientists have denounced the Bible code. Some of them have written articles worth reading. We'll review their work next.

CRITICS OF THE BIBLE CODE

Persi Diaconis, a statistician from Harvard University, was one of the original referees who reviewed the article by Witztum, Rips, and Rosenberg. He made a number of objections to the original version of the paper and suggested an elegant way to compute the probability that the alleged Bible code was just a coincidence.

Witztum, Rips, and Rosenberg say that they used his method when they rewrote their paper, and they still claim a remarkably low probability of coincidence. According to them, this proves that the Bible code is not due to chance — it was put there *intentionally*.

However, Diaconis is not convinced. According to him, Witztum, Rips, and Rosenberg used only one of the two suggestions he made. Had they used both, he believes their "remarkable results" would look a lot more ordinary.

Another major critic of the Bible code is Professor Brendan McKay, an Australian mathematician. He has posted several serious critiques on his Web site. (You'll find addresses for this and other Web sites I mention in this book's bibliography.) In an article coauthored with Dror Bar-Natan, Alec Gindis, and Arieh Levitan, he attempted to reproduce the results of Witztum, Rips, and Rosenberg using a somewhat different method. The team found very ordinary results and concluded that there is no Bible code.

In another article McKay purported to find numerous remarkable "codes" involving his own name in the Hebrew translation of Tolstoy's *War and Peace*. McKay isn't claiming that *War and Peace* contains a secret message about him; he's saying that you can find whatever you want if you know how. Doron Witztum published a response on his Web site showing the tricks McKay used to get his excellent results.

The question remains, of course, whether Witztum, Rips, and Rosenberg might have used the same tricks in their own study.

I don't believe they would have done so intentionally. Every scientist knows the danger in fiddling with the data. If you're caught doing that, your career is over.

But could they have manipulated their results unintentionally? That can happen when you're looking for a certain result. If you ignore failures and record only successes, you stand an excellent chance of seeing the pattern you want to see.

The article in *Statistical Science* took great pains to argue that the authors could not have accidentally manipulated the results. But the majority of scientists who've looked at the data are skeptical. Professor Barry Simon, an Orthodox Jewish mathematician at Cal Tech, has posted an article on his Web site explaining why.

We'll look at the arguments of the skeptics more fully in chapter 4.

OTHER WORK ON THE BIBLE CODE

In the meantime other researchers have joined the battle. The most prominent of these is Harold Gans, also an Orthodox Jew. At the time he learned of the code, Gans was a senior mathematician with twenty-eight years of experience at the National Security Agency. Like most scientists who hear of the code, his first reaction was to dismiss it as nonsense.

Unlike most scientists, Gans decided to do something about it. He programmed his home computer to do an experiment similar to that of the Israeli researchers. The experiment would, he thought, demolish the code once and for all.

Instead his experiment confirmed the work of Witztum, Rips, and Rosenberg. Gans is now director of research for Aish HaTorah (Flame of Torah), a rabbinical college in Jerusalem. Aish HaTorah is known for its popular lecture series, the Discovery Seminar, aimed at strengthening Jews in their commitment to their heritage. Part of the Discovery Seminar discusses the Bible code. Some skeptics have criticized Discovery's coverage of the topic, but I've browsed their Web site and found it a valuable resource. I've also attended a Discovery Seminar. Their lecturers appear to be trying to avoid the sensationalism that dogs the subject.

BOOKS ON THE BIBLE CODE

Speaking of sensationalists, journalist Michael Drosnin published his book *The Bible Code* in June 1997. Remarkably, it reached number three on the *New York Times* bestseller list.

Drosnin claims to have predicted the assassination of Yitzhak Rabin in November 1995 and the date of Comet Shoemaker-Levy's impact with Jupiter. He also predicts a shattering earthquake, an economic collapse, and a nuclear holocaust in the coming decade. Dramatic stuff!

But is it true?

Drosnin implied that he had a close working relationship with Eliyahu Rips for several years. However, Rips immediately issued a press release on the Internet stating that he has done no joint work with Drosnin and that he does not support Drosnin's work. Doron Witztum and Harold Gans posted their own releases saying that they don't believe the Bible code can be used to predict the future.

The August 1997 issue of *Bible Review* carried articles by Professors Ronald Hendel and Shlomo Sternberg, each denouncing Drosnin's book and the whole Bible-code movement.

There are a number of warning signals in Drosnin's book that something is amiss in his approach. He claims to know Hebrew, but native Hebrew speakers have pointed out some gross misreadings in his book. For example, the mistranslation "assassin who will assassinate" on the cover, next to Yitzhak Rabin's name. He also gets some of his facts wrong. For example, he says on page 38 that all Hebrew Bibles are letter-for-letter identical. In fact, there are differences, though remarkably few. On page 189, he says that Witztum, Rips, and Rosenberg reported odds of four in a million, but they actually reported sixteen in a million. Drosnin, who does not believe in God, concludes that space aliens dictated the Bible to Moses over three thousand years ago.

Drosnin's book is heavy on scary predictions of the future but light on hard statistical evidence. I don't know of a single scientist who has endorsed his work.

Nonetheless, Drosnin is the best known of several popular authors who have written on the Bible code. Another is Grant R. Jeffrey, an evangelical Christian author of a number of books on Bible prophecy, end-time events, and apologetic evidence, including *The Signature of God* and *The Handwriting of God,* each of which contains some chapters on the Bible code. Recently he has treated the topic more fully in *The Mysterious Bible Codes.* Jeffrey provides a broad overview of the subject, including the findings of Witztum, Rips, and Rosenberg. He believes the Bible code provides powerful evidence that God exists and inspired the Bible.

Another figure in the debate is Yacov Rambsel, a Messianic Jewish rabbi who has painstakingly searched the Hebrew Bible by hand over the last forty years, looking for hidden patterns. His first book, *Yeshua,* detailed his findings that the name "Yeshua" (that is, Jesus) is embedded in the text of nearly every prophecy considered by Christians to be messianic. (Mainstream Jews don't agree that the majority of these passages refer to the Messiah.) Rambsel followed this up with a second book, *His Name Is Jesus,* which documented his discovery of the names of many other New Testament persons in the same messianic passages. Like the Israeli researchers, Rambsel is a deeply pious man. Unlike them, he has done no scientific statistical calculations to demonstrate that these findings are anything but random chance.

Needless to say, most Jews were not amused by Rambsel's "proofs" of Jesus as the Messiah. Many Israelis have copies of Bible-code software, and some of them have countered with their own "proofs" that Jesus was a false messiah. Several well-known Bible-code researchers have also critiqued Rambsel's findings on the Internet.

In October 1997 yet another book on the Bible code appeared. *Cracking the Bible Code* is by Dr. Jeffrey Satinover, a psychiatrist currently working on a degree in physics at Yale University. This is a well-researched and entertaining book with lots of history and personal glimpses into the lives of the main players. It's the most thorough book I've seen yet on the Bible code.

Satinover believes in the code — mostly. That is, he wants to believe, but he acknowledges that the proof is not quite watertight. The book has a few minor errors (for example, in his account of Max Planck's discovery of quantum mechanics). However, Satinover is generally careful with his facts and presents a well-reasoned case for the Bible code. A weakness of the book is that he presents *all* the evidence he can find for the Bible code, and some of it is pretty thin, which dilutes the strength of his best arguments. (See his Appendix A, "Details of the New Moon.") Dr. Satinover is also the author of an article in the October 1995 issue of *Bible Review*, introducing the Bible code to many American readers.

Dr. John Weldon, an evangelical Christian, published a book in early 1998 in collaboration with Clifford and Barbara Wilson. *Decoding the Bible Code* takes a common-sense stance. Urging us not to get too excited, Weldon states that the Bible code may turn out to be true but will more likely turn out to be a hoax; the evidence isn't all in yet, but we'll find out in due time.

A healthy strain of skepticism runs through Weldon's book. What about copyist errors? What about the Kabbalistic leanings of so many Bible-code proponents? Is it logical that God would write a code so unintelligible? The book presents no new research, but it summarizes very well the state of the Bible code as of the end of 1997.

Weldon, who has a Ph.D. in comparative religion, expertly skewers a number of logical problems in Michael Drosnin's book, and he summarizes well the Internet discussions of problems in the work of Yacov Rambsel. But he is less strong on mathematical issues.

WHAT DOES IT ALL MEAN?

What shall we make of all these claims and counterclaims?

I suggest that we examine first the very best evidence for the Bible code — the work of Witztum, Rips, and Rosenberg, and the related work of Gans.

These men report the consistent results of several intriguing experiments. They claim that each experiment reveals patterns that could not happen by chance even once in fifty thousand tries.

Either they have found something extraordinary, or they are wrong, or they are lying.

I don't believe that they are lying. Mainstream scientists are occasionally caught fudging the evidence. There's one small motive to cheat — the urge to be first. But the Bible code is not mainstream science. The Bible code is weird science. Scientists don't want to be first in weird science unless they really and truly believe it. So we can be sure these men believe their results.

Either Witztum, Rips, Rosenberg, and Gans have made a subtle mistake, or they have found a real code intentionally placed in the Bible.

As I promised in chapter 1, we'll pass judgment on their results in this book. But before we can do that we need to understand their experiments in a bit more detail. It will take the whole next chapter to explain what they've done. As you'll see, their work is much more sophisticated than finding "Amy" in the alphabet.

3
—

THE SIGNATURE OF GOD?

One Friday evening a few months after I got married, the phone rang. I picked it up and said hello.

"Hi, Steve!" I didn't recognize the woman's voice, but I figured she must be a friend of my ex-roommate Steve.

"Um…no," I said. "I'm not rooming with Steve anymore. Let me get you his new number."

"Steve?" she said again.

"No, I'm Randy. Here's the —"

"No, I recognize your voice," she said. "You're Steve!" She sounded a little annoyed.

"I am?" I gave a nervous laugh. Something wasn't adding up here. Then it hit me. A prank phone call. Steve and I both loved practical jokes. It would be just like him to put one of his friends up to this.

"Steve," she continued, "will you quit teasing me? This isn't funny!" And she didn't sound like she was joking.

By now, my reality meter was beginning to tilt. Any second now I figured the theme from *The Twilight Zone* would start playing. After a long silence I tried again. "This is a prank phone call, isn't it? Steve told you to do this…right?"

"No!" Real anger colored her voice. "Steve, are you going to talk to me or are you just going to play games?"

I began feeling defensive. "Hey, I'm serious. I mean…really, I'm not Steve. Who are you anyway? How did I meet you? Are you sure you're not playing a joke?" I realized I was babbling.

"Well, fine!" she yelled. "If you're going to pretend you don't know me, I don't care. Good-bye!"

The phone slammed in my ear. I stood there, staring off stupidly into space until the recorded message from the phone company began, telling me what to do if I'd like to make a call. I hung up.

My wife, Eunice, came out of the kitchen. "What was all that about?"

I gave her a blank look. "I don't know."

I took that call more than fifteen years ago, and I still don't know. I've got several theories. Maybe it was a wrong number. Maybe it was a prank phone call. Or maybe I have a second personality named Steve and a whole different set of friends.

Eunice is quite amused by this last theory, but there doesn't seem to be much evidence for it. You can't build a strong case on one phone call. On the other hand, the other theories have problems too. If it was a wrong number, why did the woman think she recognized my voice? And if she was a prankster, she was a terrific actress. She sounded absolutely authentic.

I'll never know, but it's not really important. Life is like that. Sometimes weird things happen, and no explanation makes sense.

Which brings us to the topic of this chapter — the Great Rabbis Experiment, first reported in August 1994 in the journal *Statistical Science*. Unlike my weird phone conversation, this is important. The proponents of the Bible code claim that the results of their experiment defy natural explanation. Consequently, thousands of people believe that *this is God's signature*.

THE GREAT RABBIS EXPERIMENT

The title of the article in *Statistical Science* was extremely boring: "Equidistant Letter Sequences in the Book of Genesis." But its contents were stunning.

According to the authors — Doron Witztum, Eliyahu Rips, and Yoav Rosenberg — certain patterns had been found in the book of Genesis that suggested foreknowledge of the dates of birth and death for dozens of rabbis *who lived and died many centuries after Genesis was composed.*

THE SIGNATURE OF GOD? | 19

Publication of the article had been delayed for six years while three referees evaluated it. Not content with the original experiment, the referees insisted on numerous changes, including an analysis of a completely new set of rabbis and much stricter standards for the probability calculations.

Could the effect be due to random chance? Using the "Monte Carlo" techniques required by the referees, the authors calculated the probability of a chance effect. It turned out to be tiny, less than 0.00002. That is, better than one in fifty thousand, which is roughly the odds of having your name pulled in a random draw at a professional football game. It could happen, but it's not very likely.

The editor of *Statistical Science,* Robert Kass, then chairman of the department of statistics at Carnegie-Mellon University, prefaced the article with this note: "Our referees were baffled: Their prior beliefs made them think the Book of Genesis could not possibly contain meaningful references to modern-day individuals, yet when the authors carried out additional analyses and checks the effect persisted. The paper is thus offered to *Statistical Science* readers as a challenging puzzle."

This is academic-speak for: "I don't believe it, but the evidence is there. You figure it out, because I'm stumped."

Even while the paper was still in the review process, the experiment attracted interest in the academic community. As I mentioned in chapter 2, Harold Gans, a cryptologist at the National Security Agency, tried to debunk the claims by writing his own software on his own computer to run the same experiment. To his shock, he found that Witztum, Rips, and Rosenberg were correct. Later he tried a different experiment. This time he would match the set of rabbis to their cities of birth and death.

Remarkably, he found that the effect persisted. He computed the probability that the results could be explained by random chance. The odds were again tiny—less than one in two hundred thousand.

Witztum, Rips, and Rosenberg say that they have run another seven experiments, which produced similar results.

This makes the whole thing truly extraordinary. It's conceivable that you could have your name drawn at one football game. After all, *somebody's* name has to be drawn. But you wouldn't expect your name to be drawn week after week. If that happened, people would demand an investigation — fast.

PROOF OF GOD?

The proponents of the Bible code argue that the effect they are seeing amounts to a proof that God exists. This line of reasoning is explained at length in my favorite book on the subject, Jeffrey Satinover's *Cracking the Bible Code*. I'll paraphrase the argument in the following fourteen-point summary. Please note that this summary is my own synthesis of Satinover's chain of logic; you won't find these exact fourteen points listed anywhere in his book. Also be aware that this reasoning has been applied only to the Torah — the first five books of the Hebrew Bible.

1. An ancient Jewish tradition holds that God revealed the full text of the Torah to Moses on Mount Sinai in an unbroken sequence of letters written in black fire on a white background without punctuation or spaces.

2. Because of this tradition, Jewish scribes took extraordinary care to preserve the exact text of the Torah as copies were made through the centuries.

3. As a result of this care, the text of the Torah used by religious Jews has been maintained with amazing purity. A comparison between different copies of the five books of the Torah shows only nine differences in letters in a work of over three hundred thousand letters!

4. A widely used edition of the Torah, published by the Koren Publishing Company in Jerusalem, is assumed to be a very near copy of the original version revealed to Moses on Mount Sinai.

5. With help from computers we can look for hidden ELS words (like "Amy" in the alphabet in chapter 2) embedded in the Koren text of the Torah at equidistant letter spacings. That is, we search for words by skipping every *n* letters, where *n* is some fixed number. ELSs encoded in this way have a good chance of surviving a few copyist errors without being lost.

6. Of course we expect that a large number of ELSs would be embedded in the text purely by chance. But we are interested in ELSs that were intentionally placed there. We begin with an observation that may or may not be significant, but it serves to focus our efforts. We notice that ELSs with "related meanings" are "often" found "near" each other in the text. "Often" and "near" can be assigned precise mathematical meanings. "Related meanings" is a fuzzier concept, which we seek to clarify.

7. Based on this observation, we devise an experiment in which pairs of "related" ELSs are chosen prior to searching the text. The experiment is defined as objectively as possible so that we don't influence the outcome by choosing word-pairs that we already know will be near each other. We define in advance exactly what measure of "nearness" we will use.

8. The experiment we choose predefines a set of ELS-pairs in which one ELS is the name of a famous rabbi and the other is the date of his birth or death, using the Hebrew calendar. The list of rabbis is chosen as objectively as possible by an outside authority, and we consider only those rabbis whose dates are known accurately. All of these rabbis were born centuries after the Torah was written.

9. We can then write a computer program to measure the "nearness" of ELS-pairs and estimate the odds that our results could have occurred by chance.

10. As a check, we can run the same computer program on other texts that we do not believe to be divinely inspired.

11. It turns out that the book of Genesis shows an unusual degree of closeness between related ELS-pairs. The odds are tiny that random chance could explain the effect. Other Hebrew texts do not show the same effect. Nor do we see anything similar in rearranged texts of Genesis constructed by scrambling letters, words, or verses. We see no effect in the Samaritan version of Genesis, which is fairly close but not identical to the traditional Jewish text.

12. We conclude that the author of Genesis had knowledge of events that were future to him.

13. Since no human has such knowledge of the future, we deduce that God Himself must have provided it.

14. We surmise that God has encoded this information because He foresaw the day when modern science would begin to question the divine origin of the Torah. He also foresaw that modern science would provide computers powerful enough to detect the encoded information, thereby validating the literal letter-level revelation of the entire Torah on Mount Sinai.

DOESN'T THAT PROVE IT?

The argument looks pretty strong to a lot of people. However, problems with this "proof" have been noted consistently by two groups of people: scientists and biblical scholars — the usual suspects when there's a parade to be rained on.

If you look carefully at the complaints of each of these groups, you'll find a lot of nitpicking.

That's good.

Any far-out sounding idea *should* be nitpicked to death by smart and skeptical people. If scientists and biblical scholars eventually sign off on this thing, then maybe the Bible code is for real. And if it's all a hoax, then the folks most likely to debunk it will be the scientists and scholars.

So brace yourself for a chapter of give and take, push and pull, argument and counterargument. Some of it will seem pointless to nonacademics, but it's necessary if we want to understand the strong and weak points of the Great Rabbis Experiment. Armed with this knowledge, we'll be able to design a better experiment.

We'll get through it, or my name isn't Steve...um, I mean Randy!

4

A Look Under the Hood

Sometimes you can lie by telling the truth.

Several years ago I took my two older daughters shopping with me. Gracie was eighteen months old at the time, and Carolyn was just shy of her fourth birthday.

As I began writing a check at the checkout counter, Carolyn said in a loud voice, "Gracie, what's the square root of eighty-one?"

"Nine!" Gracie shouted out.

I finished writing the check and handed it to the cashier.

She stood there staring at my two girls.

With a modest shrug, I said, "They do that all the time." Then I glanced down the checkout line. Everybody was looking at Gracie in awe.

It took all my will power to escape to the parking lot before I collapsed in laughter.

It was all a scam, of course.

A few months earlier, we'd been teaching Carolyn her numbers. She could count to ten but not much further. One evening at supper we took turns quizzing her. "What comes after seven? What comes after eight? What comes before ten?"

At this last one, Gracie said, "Nine!" which had been the answer to the previous question.

Immediately I said, "That's right, Gracie! What's eight plus one?"

"Nine!"

We applauded loudly. "What's the square root of eighty-one?"

"Nine!"

"What's the logarithm of a billion?"

"Nine!"

After each answer, we shouted with glee, reinforcing her response.

It became a game. Every few days I'd ask her the same series of questions. She never missed. The answer was always, "Nine!"

After a few months of this, Carolyn had memorized all the questions and regularly took a turn quizzing her little sister.

That's how the trick in the supermarket was done. I told the truth — my girls played that game all the time. And yet I communicated a lie. I hadn't intended it to work out that way. It just happened.

There's a lesson to be learned from this little story. The truth isn't the truth unless it's the whole truth.

In chapter 3 we discussed a remarkable chain of logic that appears to prove that God dictated the Torah, letter by letter, in one fell swoop on Mount Sinai. This seems to fly in the face of lots of biblical scholarship over the last couple of centuries. Let's talk about that.

THE DOCUMENTARY HYPOTHESIS

According to a great many scholars today, the Torah was not written by Moses. Rather it was woven together from several documents — scholars code them as J, E, D, and P — written over a period of centuries by pious Jews. This theory, the Documentary Hypothesis, holds that the Torah was put together in final form about the time of Ezra, in the fifth century B.C. Of course, you can find conservative scholars who don't believe the Documentary Hypothesis, but few of them teach at major universities.

For a popular and understandable account of the Documentary Hypothesis, see *Who Wrote the Bible?* by Richard Elliott Friedman. The argument relies heavily on what scholars call "internal evidence" — that is, evidence within the text itself.

Many critics of the Bible code base their skepticism on a single point

— that it is absurd to look for a secret message from God in a composite document such as the Torah is alleged to be.

Of course, not all the skeptics work from the same assumptions. For example, Professors Barry Simon and Shlomo Sternberg are both Orthodox Jews who've publicly criticized the Bible code on other grounds. But some of the critics are clearly guided by a preconception that the Bible code is impossible, either because they don't believe in God or because they don't believe He was involved in writing the Bible.

Likewise, many of those who believe in the Bible code seem to be looking for an easy negation of the Documentary Hypothesis. At last! The Bible code provides internal evidence proving that only God could have written the Torah. What a remarkable result!

But remarkable results aren't enough unless the methods producing them are sound. When something sounds too good to be true, it generally is. If a car salesman claims that a model gets a thousand miles per gallon, you might want to ask for a road test before you buy it.

In this chapter, we're going to kick the tires, check the brakes, and look under the hood of the Bible code. It's a dirty job, but if we don't do it, we may wind up with a junker on our hands.

The following sections discuss major weaknesses in the fourteen-point argument we outlined in chapter 3.

DID GOD DICTATE EVERY LETTER IN THE TORAH?

Did God reveal the entire Torah to Moses on Mount Sinai, letter by fiery letter, without spaces or punctuation?

It's an extraordinary claim. Many Jews have never even heard of this letter-dictation tradition. Historically, conservative Christians have affirmed only that God inspired the words of the Bible and have assumed the spelling of the words and the timing of the revelation are irrelevant. Meanwhile, the Documentary Hypothesis simply dismisses out of hand the whole idea of God's direct authorship.

In my view, it's *possible* that God could have dictated the three hundred thousand letters of the Torah to Moses on Mount Sinai. God can do anything He wants. It just doesn't look very probable to me that He actually did such a thing.

Many of the events described in the Torah take place after the revelation on Mount Sinai. Is it reasonable to think that all those accounts in the book of Numbers of the people's complaints, rebellion, and judgment had been revealed to Moses beforehand, detail by sad detail? If they knew what was going to happen, why didn't the people shape up? Isn't it more likely that the book was written after these events and not before?

Unfortunately the opposing sides don't have enough common ground to even discuss the issue. If you take it on faith that God revealed every letter of the Torah at Sinai, then no amount of proof will dissuade you (although you'll gladly point to any available evidence that supports your faith). If you reject the possibility out of hand, then no amount of experimental evidence will change your mind (although you'll be happy to point out any flaws you might see in the experiments performed).

Certainly this all-in-one-shot theory of the Torah's revelation would be a very poor foundation on which to build a house of logic.

Please note, however, that this is *not* the foundation of Jeffrey Satinover's line of reasoning. He doesn't rely on the truth of the tradition; he uses the fact that *some Jews through the centuries have believed the tradition* to motivate his next three points regarding the extraordinary care taken to transmit the text.

To those three points we now turn.

Is the Koren Edition "Close" to the Original?

Did Jewish scribes really take extreme care in copying the Torah letter by letter for more than three millennia? How much variation exists in the texts we have received?

Satinover states that there are only nine letter-level variations among the Torah texts used by the three main ethnic streams of Jews: the Ashkenazi, Sephardi, and Yemenite communities. This is a tiny number of variants compared to the more than three hundred thousand letters of the Torah.

But Satinover is a bit optimistic here. The texts used by these religious communities aren't the only ones available, or even the best. In the August 1997 issue of *Bible Review,* Professors Ronald S. Hendel and Shlomo Sternberg discuss this point.

The text used by religious Jews today was standardized after the fifteenth-century invention of the printing press. It is close, but not identical, to the best handwritten Masoretic texts, which date to the tenth or eleventh centuries and which vary among themselves.

Professor Sternberg notes, for example, that the eleventh-century Leningrad Codex of the Torah "differs from the Koren edition…in 41 letters in Deuteronomy alone." Biblical quotations in the Talmud, the ancient Jewish collection of laws, traditions, and commentary, allow us to reconstruct parts of the text used by rabbinical authorities from A.D. 200 to 500. Sternberg says that this rabbinical text differs from the Koren edition in about three hundred letters.

Does this kill the whole idea of the Bible code?

Sternberg says it does, but the answer is not that simple. Witztum, Rips, and Rosenberg have done some experiments to see what happens when you intentionally degrade the text of Genesis. They found that the Great Rabbis Experiment still yields remarkable results when a few letters are removed at widely separated random intervals. In order to ruin the experiment, they had to delete about eighty letters from Genesis — that is, about one letter in a thousand.

But this is still not the end of the argument. In that same August 1997 issue of *Bible Review,* Dr. Ronald Hendel points out that the spellings of many Hebrew words changed over the years in that so-called vowel letters were not used in Hebrew until several centuries after the time of Moses. "So one can't count the letters in any of our Hebrew biblical manuscripts," Hendel says, "and presume that the letter count is the original. The original was shorter."

The issue Dr. Hendel raises can be a little confusing. He is referring to certain Hebrew consonants, most often *yud* and *vav,* which are usually pronounced but sometimes serve as silent placeholders for vowels. He is not referring to the "vowel points," the tiny marks to indicate vowel sounds that we see above and below letters in most texts of the Hebrew Bible today. These points were added even later than the consonants that serve as vowel placeholders. Early Hebrew was written very sparsely, without either the silent consonants or the vowel points.

Hendel doesn't provide us with an estimate of how many vowel letters have been inserted into the text. He appears to believe, like Sternberg, that even one such insertion would demolish the Bible code. As we have seen, Witztum, Rips, and Rosenberg disagree. However, if the number of insertions were more than a few hundred, it seems plausible that any code that existed in the original version of the Bible would get wiped out.

But that assumes the code was in the original. Those who believe in the Bible code believe that the code authenticates whatever version in which it is found. At least two articles posted on the Prophezine Web site have suggested that God foresaw that corruptions would occur in the text and arranged things so the Koren text would have the Bible code in it!

This is a completely ad hoc argument, but it's no more difficult to believe than the tale of the fiery letters on Mount Sinai. The reasoning goes that if God inspired every letter in the Torah and added a secret code for us to find, then He must have made sure we'd find it. Right?

That's the theory anyway.

Once again the issue can be reduced to a statement of faith. Neither the skeptics nor the believers are going to budge from their positions.

The upshot is that we have strong reasons to be highly suspicious of the Bible code, but we can't rule it out altogether. If we want proof that will satisfy both believers and skeptics, we'll need to face the alleged evidence by examining the experiment more closely.

IS THE GREAT RABBIS EXPERIMENT OBJECTIVE?

The word-pairs chosen for the Great Rabbis Experiment present numerous problems. The rabbis were selected from a reference book, Mordechai

Margalioth's *Encyclopedia of Great Men in Israel.* The original experiment took only those names supported by more than three columns of text in that book. This decision was intended as a safeguard against the authors "cherry-picking" only the names of rabbis that gave "good" results.

The referees were nevertheless cautious. They insisted on a second experiment, using the same reference book. This time rabbis were chosen whose entries had more than one and a half columns but fewer than three.

Remarkably, the results were much the same. Actually, they were a little bit better.

But wait! Could Witztum, Rips, and Rosenberg have cheated in some way? The names of the chosen rabbis had some ambiguities in spelling. Could the authors have chosen the spellings that "worked"?

According to the *Statistical Science* paper, the answer is no. Witztum, Rips, and Rosenberg say that they did not allow themselves the luxury of choosing the spellings of names. Instead they asked Professor S. Z. Havlin of the department of bibliography and librarianship at Bar Ilan University to perform the task.

The selection process has come under intense criticism by a group led by Dr. Brendan McKay. Together with several Israeli scientists, McKay closely questioned a number of decisions made by Professor Havlin that appear to be quite arbitrary.

Havlin responded with a lengthy explanation of his decisions in which he points out that he used his best professional judgment to overcome several technical problems.

For Professor Barry Simon, an Orthodox Jewish mathematician who teaches at Cal Tech, that's enough to kill the project. He's written some articles on the code for Jewish magazines, which are posted on his Web site. One of these, "The Case Against the Codes," summarizes his argument well. The fatal flaw he sees in the Bible code is that Professor Havlin had to use his judgment to choose the spellings of the names of the rabbis, and that introduces a subjective element. Professor Simon calls this "wiggle room" — the ability to pick a "good" set of data. Simon concludes that the Great Rabbis Experiment is not objective.

Brendan McKay and his comrades have pushed hard on this point. In one article posted on McKay's Web site, they showed how to cheat in this game. By playing with the spellings of the names of rabbis carefully, they cooked up a somewhat different Great Rabbis Experiment that gave poor results for the book of Genesis but excellent results for the Hebrew translation of *War and Peace.* This shows that the Great Rabbis Experiment has a disturbingly high degree of wiggle room. It has been suggested by some that Witztum, Rips, and Rosenberg *could have* influenced Havlin and *could have* cooked their experiment.

Both sides have claimed victory on this issue. The skeptics claim that the Great Rabbis Experiment is hopelessly subjective and could have been cooked; therefore, they conclude that the Bible code is a hoax. Witztum, Rips, and Rosenberg claim that they did not manipulate the results, and furthermore, they see excellent reasons for the choices Professor Havlin made; therefore, they conclude that the Bible code is real.

You can read all about it on the Web sites of McKay and Witztum. It's entertaining, but at the end of the day we're left with two camps that aren't communicating because they make different assumptions.

I'm uncomfortable with the amount of wiggle room in the Great Rabbis Experiment. I'm also uncomfortable with the notion that one can simply explain away the results of this experiment by appealing to wiggle room.

Yes, Witztum, Rips, and Rosenberg could have exploited this wiggle room. As I've already said, I don't believe they would have done so knowingly, but they could have done so unintentionally.

McKay and company have shown hard evidence that the Great Rabbis Experiment *could have* been tainted by all that wiggle room. But "could have been tainted" is different from "was tainted." We lack hard evidence that the wiggle room was actually used.

Witztum, Rips, and Rosenberg have gone to a lot of trouble to produce hard, empirical data. How can we just negate those results without other hard, empirical data?

The Great Rabbis Experiment has serious weaknesses in its design. But that doesn't prove it's wrong. No matter how many flaws the skeptics find in the experiment, the believers are always going to argue that a better experiment would still have yielded God's signature.

The real problem is that the skeptics are trying to disprove the Great Rabbis Experiment on its own fuzzy terms, attacking this or that aspect of the experiment. This is a negative approach, and it will never satisfy the believers.

We need a positive approach, a wiggle-free experiment that can prove decisively that there is or is not a Bible code. We need the experiment I've been promising since chapter 1.

DOES THE BIBLE CODE PROVE GOD EXISTS?

But first, for the sake of argument, suppose that the problems in the Great Rabbis Experiment could all be ironed out. Suppose an experiment could validate the Bible code beyond all doubt. Would this automatically persuade everybody that God wrote the Bible?

Probably not everybody.

It's possible to believe in the Bible code and not believe in God. Michael Drosnin, author of the bestseller *The Bible Code,* believes that time-traveling space aliens gave the Torah to Moses. The reason? To warn modern man of the danger of a world war and nuclear holocaust in the first decade of the new millennium.

You may think, as I do, that his theory requires a great leap of faith. But it does show that believing in the Bible code doesn't automatically lead to faith in the God of the Bible.

However, if the Bible code were proved authentic, then the choices for authorship would be considerably narrowed. How could the original author (or authors) of the Torah have known the dates of birth and death of rabbis born thousands of years later? No human could have done that. If the Bible code turns out to be true, then we have to face the possibility of extraterrestrial intelligence. Which means either God or little green men.

In either case the Bible would have an author with remarkable powers who wished to leave us clues of his existence. We will assume that he was intelligent enough to make the clues unmistakable.

But why did he bother?

Now *that* is an excellent question, and nobody has given a really good answer yet. Believers in the Bible code have often suggested that the Author left us evidence that would prove His authorship, evidence that could be discovered only in a scientific age when doubts about His existence would arise.

Pardon me for asking, but...

HAVEN'T WE HEARD THIS LINE BEFORE?

This last suggestion sounds uncomfortably like arguments in the early 1980s to support the Shroud of Turin. The shroud, it was said, contained a three-dimensional image of a crucified man. With the help of a space-age "VP-8" analyzer, you could see the 3-D image. This "proved" that the shroud held the miraculous image of Jesus, most likely imprinted there by the power of His resurrection from the dead, since no human could have created such a thing. God must have placed the image in the cloth so that modern scientists would discover it — and believe.

A number of experiments were performed, books written, lectures delivered, hopes raised.

Then permission was given for a carbon-14 test to determine the age of the cloth. Three labs independently tested tiny pieces of the cloth, and all the tests indicated that the shroud is only about seven hundred years old.

If the tests were correct, that would end the discussion. The reasonable conclusion would be that the image on the Shroud of Turin was made quite naturally by a human, although we don't know how.

Discussions like this never seem to end, however. Not long ago the shroud went back on public display in Turin, and new claims began making the rounds. A number of Web sites have sprung up, presenting evidence that the carbon-14 tests were wrong and that the shroud is genuine after all.

To my ears the arguments for the Bible code sound much like the arguments for the shroud. The same bold claims, the same exaggerations by supporters, the same fuzziness on close examination, even the same strident reactions from skeptics.

It remains to be seen whether the Bible code tests that we'll introduce in the next few chapters will be convincing. But right now, we have…

STALEMATE

You may be a Bible code believer, or you may be a skeptic. If you're a skeptic, you won't believe in the Bible code unless you see much more powerful evidence for it. If you're a believer, you won't disbelieve the code unless you see much more convincing proof against it. We have a stalemate.

For myself, the evidence of the Great Rabbis Experiment is not enough to prove the Bible code. We've seen several reasons to suspect that a subtle error has been made.

And yet…

And yet I'm reminded of the famous wager of mathematician Blaise Pascal. Pascal argued that it was rational — a good gamble, anyway — to believe in God. Let me state his reasoning this way: One can never prove absolutely that there is no God. Therefore, the probability that God exists is not zero. If God exists, then the reward for believing is infinite. If God does not exist, then the reward is zero. In either case, the cost of believing is only finite. Therefore, the shrewd gambler will believe.

The odds are against the Bible code. But if we could prove it authentic, we would have a clear and tangible reward — proof that we are not alone in the universe. That makes the matter worth pursuing a bit further, doesn't it?

On the other hand, if we can prove it's all a mistake, then we'll have a different reward — we'll silence the extravagant claims that people are making right now. That's worth the effort too.

We're almost ready to begin designing the tests that will measure if a code has been intentionally placed in the Bible. But we must be cautious, very cautious. We all have biases. Our biases can slant our reasoning and lead us astray. Even if we intend to be objective, our subconscious minds can spot patterns that aren't really there. Like "nude model Denice." Or "Amy" in the alphabet.

Before we begin our investigation, we need to understand how phony patterns can arise and what safeguards we can take to protect ourselves.

It's going to take the whole next chapter to do so, but the investment in time will pay off richly.

5

THE BIAS PROTECTION PLAN

It's easy to find remarkable patterns in the Bible, patterns that "couldn't possibly arise by chance." The temptation is to claim that these patterns prove that something unusual is going on. Often they do not.

Let's look at an "amazing pattern" that's well-known among Bible-code aficionados. If you look at the Hebrew text of Genesis, you'll find the word "Torah" spelled out at intervals of 50 letters, starting with the very first word of the book. The probability would seem tiny that exactly this ELS would occur at exactly this location and exactly this skip.

Isn't that remarkable? Well, no. Remember "Amy" in the alphabet? If you go to a Discovery Seminar (the popular Jewish lecture series I mentioned earlier), you'll see examples like this one picked to shreds. Let's see why.

"Torah" is spelled with four common letters in Hebrew. It's not surprising that you can find this word spelled out at a number of different locations in the Torah at a number of different skips. Given that there's a *tav* in the first word of Genesis, the odds are greater than 5 percent of finding the other three letters of "Torah" at a skip less than 100! That's *5 percent,* not "one in three million" as some people have claimed for this ELS.

Is there anything special about the number 50? Not really. Most people would be just as happy to find this ELS at a skip of 49 or 75 or 100. True, Jewish numerologists could probably find some meaning to attach to the number 50. But they would be attaching this meaning in hindsight.

That's the flaw. If we found the ELS at a skip of 93, we could just as easily find a meaning for that.

Here's the sequence of events:

Somebody finds the word "Torah" at some location and some interval.

Then they attach significant meaning to that particular location and interval.

This is exactly the wrong sequence! What if the word had been found at some other location? At some other interval? You can bet they would assign just as much meaning to it. And what they would be doing is *post-dicting* rather than *predicting*. (I know, I know; "postdicting" is not a word. I'm only using it to annoy my know-it-all word processor.)

Now please understand that this postdiction — attaching meaning in hindsight — is not, in principle, a bad thing. Scientists do it all the time when they look at data and try to come up with a theory to explain that data.

The bad thing is to stop there. A theory is not much use if you can only use it to explain data you already have. A theory is useful only *if you can then use it to predict something new.* Hindsight has to lead to foresight. If the Bible code is real — if the Hebrew Bible is filled with hidden messages — then a scientific analysis of patterns in the text should lead to new patterns. For example, the first version of the Great Rabbis Experiment led to the second one, which led to a third one by Harold Gans. All of the leading code researchers will tell you that the "Torah" code we discussed is a meaningless coincidence.

Here's a fundamental question: Who *predicted* that the word "Torah" would be found at a skip of 50 letters, starting with the first word of Genesis? What was the basis for that prediction?

The answer is that nobody predicted it explicitly. Instead, somebody made a fuzzy implicit prediction that some interesting word would be found at some skip. (This was a pretty safe prediction. With thousands of possible words and many possible skips, something was bound to turn up.) Then, after finding "Torah" at a skip of 50, somebody did some sloppy postdiction and calculated the probability of finding exactly that word at exactly that skip. This is a lot like laying an exacta-bet at the racetrack after the race has been run. It's interesting that a similar "Torah" ELS is found in Exodus. But if it hadn't been found, which theory would have crumbled? None. And what prediction can we make for Leviticus, Numbers, and Deuteronomy? None that works.

WHY IS PREDICTION SO IMPORTANT?

You may be asking why it's so important that something be predicted. After all, if something remarkable has happened, then why should we care whether somebody predicted it or merely postdicted it?

I'll answer that with a question. How do you know if something remarkable *has* happened?

When we say that something is remarkable, we mean that it was very unlikely and yet it happened anyway.

We can express this idea in a precise mathematical way. When we say that something is very unlikely, we mean that it has a very low probability. Mathematicians define probability as a number between 0 and 1 (like a batting average in baseball). A probability of 0 means that the event could not possibly occur. A probability of 1 means that the event absolutely must occur.

Take a quarter out of your pocket and flip it, letting it land on the floor. About half the time it should land heads up, and half the time it should land tails up. Once in a blue moon it might land on its edge.

We express this mathematically as follows. The probability of landing heads up is almost exactly a half; so is the probability of landing tails up. The probability of landing on the edge is almost exactly 0. The combined probability of landing either heads *or* tails *or* on the edge is 1.

So when we say that a remarkable event occurred, we mean that the probability of the event is very, very close to 0.

Now it's easy to estimate the probabilities of some events. We guessed the probability of heads to be a half. Likewise for tails. But what's the exact probability of the coin landing on its edge?

Less than one in a million? Less than one in a billion? How can you know? What assumptions are you making?

Suppose you and I are idly flipping coins and by chance one coin does land on its edge. Should we be surprised? Sure. Should we be impressed? Not really. Weird stuff happens.

Now suppose we're idly flipping coins, and *I tell you* that the next one will definitely land on the edge. I flip the coin, and…it lands on its edge! Wow!

That is the difference prediction makes.

Babe Ruth hit a home run in the 1932 World Series against Charlie Root, a pitcher for the Chicago Cubs. That wasn't such a big deal. The Babe had hit a lot of home runs in his career. But this homer was different. According to legend, just before the pitch Ruth pointed with his bat out to center field, in precisely the direction he actually would hit the ball.

This was the Babe's famous "Called Shot." Some sportswriters will tell you it's a myth, but others swear that it happened. No matter. The story is special because of the prediction. Without the prediction, it's just another home run.

So prediction is crucial. Now let's tackle the question from a more technical angle.

When something remarkable happens, it's all too easy to make a naive estimate of the probability.

Here's an example that a physicist friend, Jay R. Hill, pointed out to me. You may recall from high school math that the number represented by the Greek letter π (indicating the ratio of a circle's circumference to its diameter) starts out as 3.14159 and goes on forever without any discernible pattern. If you look at the first thousand digits of the number π, you'll find a sequence of six 9s in a row. Here are some of the digits:

8 6 4 0 3 4 4 1 8 1 5 9 8 1 3 6 2 9 7 7 4 7 7 1 3 0 9
9 6 0 5 1 8 7 0 7 2 1 1 3 4 <u>9 9 9 9 9 9</u> 8 3 7 2 9 7 8

There they are! Six 9s in a row! What are the odds of that?

Suppose we try to naively calculate the odds. Each digit of π is equally likely to be one of the ten digits from 0 through 9. Since each possibility is equally likely, the probability that a given digit will be a 9 is one in ten, or one-tenth, that is, 0.1.

Now what's the probability that two 9s in a row will show up? Clearly, there are a hundred possible ways to choose two digits at random, so the odds are one in a hundred, 0.01.

Continuing on, the probability of three 9s in a row is one in a thousand, 0.001. And the probability of six 9s in a row is one in a million, 0.000001.

Wow! Odds of one in a million! That must mean something, right?

Well, not exactly.

For one thing, this remarkable sequence was found beginning at digit number 762. Did somebody predict that the sequence would start there? No. If we'd found them at digit number 761 or digit number 32, we'd have been just as happy, wouldn't we? That is, we'd still consider the sequence "remarkable."

So there are at least 762 remarkable "one in a million" events that would have caught our attention. Of these, 761 didn't happen. One did. What's so remarkable about that?

You may argue that the remarkable thing is that we found this "one in a million" sequence so early. But within the first thousand digits of π, there are about a thousand different ways that could have happened, depending on which digit you started at. So the odds of it happening this early are actually a thousand times more than one in a million — that is, one in a thousand.

That still seems fairly unusual, but suddenly it's not quite so amazing. But there's more.

We found six 9s in a row. But what if we'd found six 0s? Or six 7s? We'd have been just as happy, wouldn't we?

You may now argue that the remarkable thing is that we found *any* sequence of six repeated digits so early. But the odds of that happening are ten times as high as the odds of finding six 9s. So our "one in a million" event really has a probability of one in a hundred. And that's not such a big deal, is it?

We could continue, but the trend is clear. Our first naive estimate of probability for this event was wrong. Amazingly wrong.

What went awry?

Here's the procedure we followed.

We found a particular remarkable sequence (six 9s in a row) at a particular location (starting with digit number 762).

We then calculated the probability *of that exact event.*

We found that the odds of finding six 9s starting at digit number 762 are one in a million.

That result, however, was meaningless, as we discovered under closer scrutiny. It was an example of postdiction. To quote that famous philosopher Garfield the Cat, "Big fat hairy deal."

But suppose a mathematician worked out a theory of π that predicted a sequence of exactly six 9s at that exact location. Suppose she then looked up the answer and found that her theory was correct. Suppose she used the same theory to predict other long sequences of digits at other locations, and those predictions turned out to be true too.

If all that happened, then we'd be on to something.

Why?

Because we *predicted* some highly unlikely results. And we did it time after time after time.

That's what science is all about — making predictions that turn out to be true. A good scientific theory is a lot like a biblical prophet. Its predictions come true. And like the biblical prophets, if a theory makes a wrong prediction, it has to be killed.

In science, it's not quite possible to stone a theory, of course. What usually happens is that the theory gets improved in some way, so that it correctly postdicts the event that it had wrongly predicted before.

But then the new and improved theory has to be tested by making new predictions that turn out to be true. It's not enough to merely postdict the old. A theory isn't any good until it can make testable predictions that turn out to be true.

Forcing ourselves to make predictions is our protection against bias. Not only does prediction protect me against your biases, it also protects me against mine and you against yours. Prediction separates the men from the boys, the prophets from the profiteers, the scientists from the quacks.

THE PROBLEM WITH THE GREAT RABBIS EXPERIMENT

Now what does all this talk about postdiction and prediction have to do with the Bible code?

Plenty.

The scientific evidence for the Bible code rests on the Great Rabbis Experiment. According to the authors of that experiment, they performed the following scientific experiment:

1. They chose the names of a certain group of rabbis and looked up their birth dates and death dates. They predicted that the names and dates of those rabbis would be found as ELSs in unusually close proximity.

2. They then performed the experiment and found that the prediction was true.

On the surface it looks like they followed proper scientific method.

As we saw in chapter 4, however, the experiment had some wiggle room. By choosing "good" spellings of rabbis' names, the scientists could theoretically change the outcome of the experiment. But that would effectively be a postdiction, since you have to do an initial experiment in order to know which spellings are "good." That's why the experiment looks suspicious to most scientists.

Please note: There are no math errors in the paper by Witztum, Rips, and Rosenberg. But the procedure they describe is sensitive to wiggle room — more sensitive than it should be.

BEYOND THE GREAT RABBIS EXPERIMENT

All right, then, the Great Rabbis Experiment appears to be flawed. Because of its wiggle room, it could be partly a postdiction.

Are we stuck with it as our only proof?

No. We can do better, and we will do better — here, in this book. The skeptics claim that the alleged Bible code is random nonsense. The believers claim that it is an intentionally encoded message. Let's talk about the ideal experiment we could run to distinguish between these two choices. We'll make four requirements:

1. It must be natural. In other words, it must use measurements that are already commonly used by scientists (whether or not these look natural to laypeople).

2. The experiment must have no wiggle room.

3. The measurements must be able to distinguish between random data and an intentional message.

4. The measurements must be tested on several nonbiblical texts to demonstrate the sort of results we ought to expect when there is no Bible code. The results from one text should be used to predict the results for other texts.

Once we've got such a set of measurements, we'll be ready to test the reality of the Bible code. The logic will follow the usual logic of a scientific experiment.

1. Assume that the text of the Hebrew Bible has no Bible code in it, just like the other texts we've examined.

2. Based on that assumption, predict the results of our measurements on the Hebrew Bible.

3. Run the tests on the Hebrew Bible. If the measurements agree with our predictions, then we conclude that there is no evidence for the Bible code. If the measurements disagree with our predictions, then we conclude that assumption number 1 is wrong — therefore the Bible code is real.

That's the plan. In the next seven chapters, we'll develop our tests. We'll begin by showing how to catch a cheat — intentional or not.

6

To Catch a Cheat

Jeff clattered the three dice noisily in his hands and flung them into the box. "Six, six, five!" he crowed. "Excellent!"

It was a summer evening before my senior year in high school, and several of the guys were playing the board game *Risk*. The goal is to conquer the world. Jeff had ten armies in the Middle East attacking my two armies in Egypt. Normally, that kind of attack was a sure thing. But that night I was rolling abnormally well.

In *Risk* the attacker can roll up to three dice, but the defender can roll at most two. You match the attacker's top dice against the defender's. Ties go to the defender.

I picked up the two white dice, shook them hard in my hands, shouted my favorite incantation, "Oonga, Boonga!" and let fly. Six, six. The only combination that could beat Jeff's roll.

Jeff growled under his breath and removed two of his armies. He rolled again quickly. Six, five, two — another "excellent" roll.

I hollered, "Oonga, Boonga!" and rolled my dice. Six, five!

Jeff wiped away two more of his armies and rolled his dice. "Most excellent! Six, six, six!" His luck was uncanny this evening.

But mine was better. With another "Oonga, Boonga!" I threw a pair of sixes.

Jeff swept off two of his armies, fixed me with a cold stare, and decided to attack Doug in the Ukraine.

As I look back on it now, I remember clearly that we rolled many more sixes than ones. Were we lucky? Was it due to our wacky incantations, like "Oonga, Boonga"?

Or did we cheat?

Most of us used a similar method in rolling the dice. My ritual never varied. First, I'd arrange the dice on the table to show all sixes. I'd scoop them up, shake them in a tight grip — making lots of noise but not really mixing them at all — and send them skidding across the box into the corner. "Oonga, Boonga!"

With some practice, it was easy to roll at least a six-four pair every time. When I was hot, as I was during Jeff's ill-fated African campaign, I was unbeatable on defense.

I think we all suspected that we were cheating, but we had no way to prove it, and none of us wanted to admit it.

Had I known then of the powerful statistical methods available, I could have proved my friends were cheating. But of course, I'd have indicted myself at the same time, so there wouldn't have been much incentive.

Which brings me to the topic of this chapter — randomness and how to detect it.

ALL ABOUT RANDOMNESS

When you throw the dice, the results are supposed to be random. This means that you should roll about the same number of ones as sixes or threes or any other number.

Likewise, when you flip a coin, you expect about the same number of heads as tails.

Notice that I say "about the same number" and not "exactly the same number."

Why?

Because getting the same number is not very likely and is often impossible. Flip a coin three times. You might get three heads, or you might get three tails. More likely, you'll get two heads and one tail or vice versa. But you'll never get one and a half heads and one and a half tails. That's impossible.

Now flip a coin 100 times. It's possible that you'll get 50 heads and 50 tails. But there are plenty of other possibilities. You might get 51 heads and 49 tails, or you might get 52 heads and 48 tails.

Whatever you get, the results are likely to be near 50. You could get 100 heads and no tails, but that's an extremely remote possibility.

All of this was analyzed a long time ago by mathematicians. What they've found is very interesting (and very relevant to our question of cheating).

Imagine that every reader of this book flips a coin 100 times and mails me the results. (Please don't do this — your time is valuable.) Most of your results would be near 50 heads and 50 tails. What does "near" mean? There's a mathematical formula that defines "near" precisely. (For the details, see Appendix A on my Web site. "A Final Note" at the back of this book explains how.) The answer for this particular case is 5. I can predict that about two-thirds of you will get a result between 45 and 55 heads. We generally write this as "50 heads, plus or minus 5."

Here we call 50 the "expected value," and we call 5 the "spread."

To summarize, the expected value tells you the average number of heads to expect in a set of random trials. The spread tells you about how much variation you'll see.

Mathematicians tell us that practically all the results will fall within a range of plus or minus three times the spread. In our case, three times the spread is 15, so I'd expect most readers to tell me they got between 35 and 65 heads.

That's actually a fairly broad range. Now here's an interesting fact. If you flipped the coin 10,000 times, instead of 100, the expected number of heads would increase to 5,000. But the spread would increase only to 50.

So almost all of you would report that you got a number between 4,850 and 5,150.

That's a remarkably small spread compared to the number of flips! As you flip the coin more and more times, the relative spread decreases. Mathematicians call this the Law of Large Numbers. We can use this law to detect whether a process is random or not. It's exactly the tool we need for catching cheats in dice. More important, it's one of the tools we'll use in this book to check whether the "signature of God" is authentic.

Now let's apply these ideas to show exactly how to prove someone is cheating. First, we'll consider the problem of coin flipping, then we'll tackle the question of dice throwing.

CHEATING AT COIN FLIPPING

Suppose I tell you that I flipped a coin 10,000 times and got 5,010 heads. Should you believe that my coin is fair?

The answer is yes. In 10,000 flips, we expect to see 5,000 heads, plus or minus 50. My result was only 10 more than the expected value — well within the spread. There's no reason at all to suspect any cheating.

But suppose I tell you that I flipped that coin 10,000 times and saw 5,100 heads. My result is 100 more than the expected value. That's twice the spread! Should you still believe the coin is fair?

The answer is "probably." Most of the time, a fair coin won't yield results that far above the expected value, but it can happen about once in 45 times. The usual approach of statisticians is to give the benefit of the doubt in cases like this. Your wisest course would be to ask me to flip the coin another 10,000 times and tell you the results.

Finally, suppose I tell you that I flipped the coin 10,000 times and saw 5,500 heads. Should you believe the coin is fair?

No way!

I'd be reporting a result that's 500 heads more than the expected value. But the spread is only 50! The deviation is 10 times the spread, and the odds of that happening by chance with a fair coin are almost nil. We can look up the probability in a mathematical table. It's about 8 in a trillion trillion.

To give you an idea how small the odds are, consider this. The average IQ is supposed to be 100, plus or minus about 16. So 10 times the spread is 160. Do you know anyone with an IQ of 260?

I didn't think so. Marilyn vos Savant has been listed in the *Guinness Book of World Records* as having an IQ of 228, the highest ever recorded. I regularly read her column, and I agree that she is one very smart lady. But her IQ exceeds the average by 128, which is only 8 times the spread.

In the rest of this book, we're going to use the standard language for this sort of calculation, the so-called Z-score. We're going to measure results of random experiments in terms of multiples of the spread. If we report a result that's one multiple of the spread *more* than the expected value, we'll call that a Z-score of 1. If the result is one multiple of the spread *less* than the expected value, the Z-score is -1.

So Marilyn vos Savant's IQ has a Z-score of 8, because she beats the average by 8 multiples of the spread.

And my alleged coin-flipping experiment, which beat the expected value by 10 multiples of the spread, has a Z-score of 10.

For random experiments like coin flipping, the larger the Z-score, the more unlikely it is. Z-scores are distributed according to the infamous bell-shaped curve. A Z-score larger than 3 (or a Z-score less than -3) happens barely once in a thousand times. If you see a Z-score of 3 or so, it isn't automatic proof of foul play, but it is grounds for suspicion. A Z-score more than 5 is highly unlikely. The mathematicians tell us that the odds are about 3 in 10 million that you'd get a result so far above the expected value. Scientists call such Z-scores "outliers."

Outliers demand an explanation. In the case of coin flipping, we can think of a few possible reasons for outliers:

1. The coin is not a fair coin.

2. The person flipping the coin has extraordinary control in the art of coin flipping. (Some magicians have mastered this skill, which takes months to learn.)

3. The person recording the coin flips failed to record the results accurately.

But what about the case of the delightful Ms. vos Savant? She has a Z-score of 8! The odds of seeing such a high Z-score are less than one in a million billion. Fewer than ten billion people live on this planet. So Ms. vos Savant's IQ is an outlier. How do we explain that?

We don't really have to. The causes of intelligence are not all that well understood, but I would bet they're not completely random. So the mathematical model probably doesn't perfectly fit IQ scores.

However, the mathematical model does fit coin-flipping experiments exceedingly well, and that's what we're interested in here.

We've answered the question on how to catch a cheat at coin flipping. All we have to do is use the math found in Appendix A on my Web site to calculate the Z-score. If it's less than 2, then there is no reason to suspect cheating. If Z is between 2 and 3, we ask for another experiment. If Z is greater than 3, we start asking hard questions about the coin, the person flipping it, and the person recording the results.

A coin is simple. It lands either heads or tails, so we only have to count the heads and we automatically know the number of tails. As scientists say, we have one "degree of freedom" — the number of heads. But dice have six sides, not two. That's not so simple.

How do we detect cheating at dice?

CHEATING AT DICE

The extra wrinkle here is that each die has six faces. So in order to keep track of results, we have to count how many 1s, 2s, 3s, 4s, and 6s were rolled. Actually, we only have to count five of these categories, since we can then compute the sixth. We say that dice have five degrees of freedom. In practice most people count all six, but it turns out to be important that we don't have to. If the die is fair, then each of the six faces should come up with equal probability. If you roll the dice 600 times, you'd expect to see about 100 occurrences of each face.

In our statistical language, the "expected frequency" of each face is 100. Using the formula (A6) in Appendix A, the spread would be about 9.13.

Now suppose you suspect somebody of cheating at dice. Can you prove it?

If you have enough time, the answer is yes!

Just watch them throw the dice, record the results, and compute the Z-scores. If you collect enough data, you'll eventually have the evidence you need.

In fact, let's try it right now — on me.

Oonga, Boonga!

We're going to do an experiment to see how good I am at cheating with dice. I'll make 200 throws, each time rolling three dice, for a total of 600 dice rolled. I'll record the results and then we'll see if there's enough evidence to convict me. Here goes…

Okay, I'm back. Whew! Let me tell you, I had some pretty hot rolls there. Lots of 6s — just what any *Risk* player wants. I think I rolled a bit better back in high school, but not much. Maybe it's because I didn't say, "Oonga, Boonga," this time. Never mind that, though. I feel like heading out to Las Vegas to make my fortune.

Of course you don't want to take just my word for it. You'll want to look at the data for yourself. Very well, I'll run my data through a little program that tabulates the results, and then we'll display the numbers in Table 6.1. The left column lists the six faces on a die, the numbers 1 through 6. The second column shows how many of each face I actually rolled. The third column shows the Z-scores, using an expected count of 100 and a spread of 9.128709. Now, if I'm a cheat, the row labeled "6" ought to have a high Z-score.

Number	Count	Z-Score
1	91	-0.986
2	106	0.657
3	110	1.095
4	98	-0.219
5	100	0.000
6	95	-0.548

TABLE 6.1: Z-SCORES FOR DICE-CHEATING EXPERIMENT.

Holy cow! Do you see what I see?

Every one of those Z-scores is perfectly normal! I'm not a cheat! I didn't even score the *expected number* of 6s! If you don't mind, I'm going to cancel those reservations in Las Vegas. Frankly, it just wouldn't pay.

There's a lesson here. Several lessons, in fact.

First, our emotions can fool us. While I was rolling the dice, I told my wife what remarkable skill I still have, even twenty years later. It really felt like I was seeing lots of 6s. Of course I was looking for 6s. I didn't notice all those 3s, because a *Risk* player never really notices 3s.

Second, it's harder to cheat than I thought.

Third, numbers don't lie. Just look at all those Z-scores. After all these years, my guilty conscience is now clean.

Actually, all those Z-scores can get to be a problem. It's rather annoying that there are six of them. In the case of coin flipping, we only reported one number, the Z-score. Now we have to report six of them. What if the dice had 100 sides? Or 1,000? That's a lot of numbers to look at. Because of that, statisticians developed another tool for studying things like dice.

CHI-SQUARED — FOR MULTIPLE Z-SCORES

When you have more than one Z-score to look at, you can combine them into a single new score. Mathematicians call it the "chi-squared" value, which is a fancy name for a simple idea. Here's what you do. Take all those Z-scores and square them (that is, multiply each one by itself). Then add up the results. The total is the chi-squared value. Table 6.2 shows how you do this for the dice experiment we just looked at. In this case, the chi-squared value is 2.952.

What the chi-squared statistic does is to sum up the average amount of deviation from the expected values of a group of numbers. The higher the

Number	Count	Z-Score	Z-Squared
1	91	-0.986	0.972
2	106	0.657	0.432
3	110	1.095	1.200
4	98	-0.219	0.048
5	100	0.000	0.000
6	95	-0.548	0.300
		Chi-squared:	*2.952*
		Probability:	*0.707*

TABLE 6.2: CALCULATING THE CHI-SQUARED VALUE FOR THE DICE-CHEATING EXPERIMENT.

value of chi-squared, the more deviation we're observing, and the more surprised we ought to be. We always expect some variation, of course. We expect the chi-squared value to be roughly equal to the number of degrees of freedom, give or take a few. Remember that our dice had five degrees of freedom. Therefore, a chi-squared of 2.952 falls well within our expectations for what random chance should produce.

There are mathematical tables available to estimate the probability that the chi-squared we have observed is due to random chance. (See Appendix B on my Web site for the details.) Table 6.2 displays the probability for our experiment, which is 0.707. You should be highly suspicious when this number is less than 0.001. If the probability is larger than 0.01, then consider your experiment to be random. If the probability is between 0.001 and 0.01, redo the experiment. Clearly, my dice-throwing results are entirely explainable by random chance. In other words, *I can't cheat worth beans.*

Chi-squared is a powerful tool! Already, we've used it to acquit me of a crime I didn't commit twenty-plus years ago.

Now let's use it to expose a real case of cheating. I'm going to roll the dice again, but I'll make two changes. First, I'm not going to try to manipulate the dice. I'll just roll them any old way I feel like it. However, I'm going to cheat in a different way, by recording only the results that look good to a *Risk* player. So I'll roll three dice at a time, but I won't record the results unless there's at least one 6 in the roll. Here goes…

Twenty minutes later I'm back. Here are the results in Table 6.3.

Number	Count	Z-Score	Z-Squared
1	64	-3.944	15.552
2	73	-2.958	8.748
3	70	-3.286	10.800
4	67	-3.615	13.068
5	85	-1.643	2.700
6	241	15.446	238.572
		Chi-squared:	*289.440*
		Probability:	*1.86E-60*

TABLE 6.3: CALCULATING THE CHI-SQUARED VALUE FOR A BETTER DICE-CHEATING EXPERIMENT.

The results here are stunningly different. Not one of the Z-scores is less than 1. Most of them are up around 3 or higher, which is usually a sign of hanky-panky with the numbers. And the Z-score for the count of 6s is more than 15, which is huge.

Notice the fourth column. When the Z-score is large, the square of Z is really large. The result is a value of chi-squared that goes off the charts. We expected a chi-squared of 5 or so. We got a chi-squared of more than 289! The probability of such a large chi-squared is so tiny, it has to be shown in scientific notation. It's less than a billionth of a billionth of a billionth of…oh, never mind.

This is an important result. It tells us how easy it is to cheat by simply ignoring data. In my case, I ignored every throw that didn't have at least one 6 among my three dice. I wound up ignoring just a bit more than half of the throws. This allowed me to record more than twice as many 6s as random chance would have allowed. The result was to send the chi-squared value skyrocketing. With the chi-squared test, a little cheating goes a long way.

Now all this arithmetic can be applied to the Great Rabbis Experiment. In chapter 16, we'll work through a chi-squared analysis of the results of that experiment. If we discover that the results just can't be due to random chance, that leaves only two real possibilities:

1. God did it (or space aliens, for those who follow that school of thought).

2. Witztum, Rips, and Rosenberg have somehow ignored data that they shouldn't have. They may have done this knowingly or unknowingly, or their computer program may be in error.

We intend to develop a new approach in this book — a method very different from the Great Rabbis Experiment. The chi-squared test is going to play a major role in this method. It will take a couple more chapters to fully explain how this will work, but we can get started right now.

A FIRST TEST

We've discussed how to measure cheating in random experiments like coin flipping and dice throwing. Now let's use our ideas on a real text. The text we're going to use is a strange one. We're going to look at the digits of the number π.

We talked about π in chapter 5. It starts out 3.14159 and goes on for-ever with no visible pattern. In other words, the digits appear to be random. You can find numerous Web pages that display π to millions of digits, or even billions. We don't need that many. The sequence we'll be using has just under 50,000 digits (49,981, to be exact), which is about half the number of characters we'll find in the longest Bible texts we'll analyze later.

In this chapter, the only question we'll ask is whether the digits of π are randomly distributed. Now each digit must be one of the numbers: 0, 1, 2, 3, 4, 5, 6, 7, 8, or 9. So there are ten possibilities. If the digits are ran-domly distributed, then we ought to see about the same number of each in the text of π we selected.

I've written some software to count the digits and perform the chi-squared analysis. (See "A Final Note" at the back of this book for directions on how to get this software from the Internet so you can run it on your own computer.)

We expect to see each digit about 4,998 times, plus or minus 67. Since we have ten possible digits, we have nine degrees of freedom for the chi-squared analysis. We therefore expect a chi-squared value of about 9. Here are the results in Table 6.4:

Digit	Count	Z-Score	Z-Squared
0	5029	0.461	0.212
1	5053	0.819	0.670
2	4863	-2.014	4.058
3	4947	-0.762	0.580
4	5008	0.148	0.022
5	5050	0.774	0.599
6	5016	0.267	0.071
7	4976	-0.330	0.109
8	5030	0.476	0.226
9	5009	0.163	0.026
		Chi-squared:	*6.573*
		Probability:	*0.681*

TABLE 6.4: CHI-SQUARED ANALYSIS OF THE FIRST 49,981 DIGITS OF π.

The chi-squared value is 6.573, well within the expected value. The computed probability that this is due to random chance is 0.681 — in other words, more likely than not. We conclude that the digits of π appear randomly distributed, at least when we use this simple approach. (In the next few chapters, we'll see that there's more to the story, but π will continue to pass all tests for randomness.)

GOD'S SIGNATURE IN π?

In 1987, Carl Sagan published *Contact,* an interesting novel that recently made it to the big screen. As usual, he had many tantalizing ideas. One of them was the question of what sort of signature God might have left for us, had He chosen to do so. One possibility is to embed in π a long string of digits that would jump out at us — a pattern that would be immensely unlikely to happen by chance.

We're not talking about something trivial like the six 9s we saw in chapter 5. We explained that away with little effort. A six-character sequence is just too short. In Sagan's book, the heroine found a string of hundreds of 0s and 1s in the "base-11 representation of π." Never mind what that means exactly. Hundreds of such digits in a row would be highly improbable. And when Sagan's heroine printed this string out as a square grid, the 1s made a circle in a sea of 0s!

Now that sort of thing would make a scientist's jaw drop down on the floor. Yes, really. The probability of that kind of event happening by chance, as described in the book, is incredibly low. Imagine listening to Professor Sagan saying, "A billionth of a billionth of a billionth…" several hundred times, and you get the picture. Remember that cosmologists tell us there have been fewer than a billion billion seconds since the Big Bang.

Now, of course, this is all fiction. In real life the digits of π haven't turned up anything so beautiful. But if they did, you can bet scientists would start asking who put it there. That is, *Who* put it there.

We scientists are a skeptical crew. That's what you pay us for — to ask hard questions. But there are ways to impress us. If the characters in the text of the Hebrew Bible truly turn out to have significant patterns like the one I just described, we'll be interested.

But the patterns must be really good. I don't know of a single scientist who has endorsed the claims made by Michael Drosnin in *The Bible Code*. And the majority of us haven't bought into the Great Rabbis Experiment either, although that one at least gets our attention.

What we want is something dazzling. Something extraordinary. Something a lot better than "Amy" in the alphabet. Give us a pattern with a probability of a billionth of a billionth of a billionth…, and we'll agree that the Hebrew Bible carries the signature of an Author.

Is such a pattern even possible?

Of course it is, as we'll find when we study *The Cat in the Hat*, coming up next. Oonga, Boonga!

7

AN INFINITE NUMBER
OF MONKEYS

"If an infinite number of monkeys played with an infinite number of type-writers, one of them would write all the works of Shakespeare."

Ever heard that one? I must have heard it from a dozen people.

And they're all wrong.

The correct statement is that if an infinite number of monkeys played with an infinite number of typewriters, *an infinite number of them* would write all the works of Shakespeare.

The fun part would be working through the slush pile.

What's a slush pile? No, it's not a pile of…um, animal by-products. "Slush pile" is the most hated term in the publishing industry.

When unknown writers send their unrequested treasures to publishing houses, their work often languishes for months in the slush pile, a mountain of manuscripts waiting to be evaluated by somebody — anybody — when there's a free moment. Writers hate the slush pile because their work can sit there for ages, unread. Editors hate the slush pile because the quality of writing isn't usually all that high.

Now imagine some poor intern assigned to read through the slush pile of the infinite number of monkeys. Picture her sitting in her cube at 2 A.M., bored out of her bones, bad coffee drilling tunnels through her veins, rejecting monkey-manuscript after monkey-manuscript. Suddenly, she sits bolt upright, a wild look of disbelief in her eye. *Hamlet!* The full text — written by a monkey!

Our heroine pulls out her *Complete Works of William Shakespeare* and compares the two copies, line by line. Dazzled, she reaches Hamlet's soliloquy:

"To be or not to be, that is the questiobdfhtaywrtyglsaoigusgfhash."

Rats!

Did I mention that this intern would see this exact same manuscript an infinite number of times?

Now I'm not just a writer, I'm a computer geek. We geeks often say, "Anything people can do, computers can do better." Okay, not quite everything. My computer can print this book in about thirty minutes, which is slightly faster than I can type it. But there's no way my computer could write this book.

But a computer could easily be taught to search for text. Not just any text. English text. Or German. Or Hebrew.

To be more precise, it could be taught to look for text with the characteristics of English or German or Hebrew. You'd still need to ask a human to check whether the text made sense, but it'd be a great way to thin out the slush pile. Most slush piles, anyway. Unfortunately, you can thin out an infinite slush pile all you want; it'll still be infinite.

In this chapter we're going to show a simple way to program a computer to guess whether a given text is written in English or German or Hebrew or any other language that uses a phonetic alphabet.

You already know the principle if you've ever played a certain common children's game.

HOW TO WIN AT HANGMAN

Remember Hangman? You think up a word and draw a space for each letter in the word.

Then the other players take turns guessing letters. If they name a letter that happens to be in your chosen word, you write that letter in its correct position. Otherwise you draw another body part on a sketch of someone being hanged.

Now if *you're* the one guessing letters, which do you start with? *z? q? v?*

Generally not. The most common letters in the English language are *e, t, a, o, n, r, i, s, h, d, l,* and *f,* in that order. If you guess those letters first, you stand a pretty good chance of filling in some letters before your neck has to make like a bungee cord.

That's the strategy I usually take when I'm on the gallows. On the other hand, when I'm the hangman, I choose a word made up of letters far down the list. One of my favorites is "syzygy." Some of my friends have worked their way through the *entire* alphabet, stumped by that *z*. It's kind of fun to hang someone *twice* on a single word. If you pull this stunt, keep a dictionary handy to prove that "syzygy" is really an English word and not something you made up.

Code-breakers and other devious people exploit these ideas when breaking simple ciphers — the kind children like to make up, in which each "secret symbol" stands for exactly one letter in the alphabet. These ciphers are easy to break if you have enough encoded text.

What you do is count how frequently each of the "secret symbols" occurs in the code. Then you compare these frequencies to the known frequencies of letters in normal English. The letter *e* occurs about 13 times in every 100 letters of normal English text; *t* occurs about 10 times; *a* and *o* each occur about 8 times. The frequencies for all the letters of the alphabet have long ago been tabulated by code-breakers. (If you read the appendices on my Web site, you'll know that I really mean the letter *probabilities,* not frequencies. There's a technical difference. Here in the main text of this book, I'll use the two terms interchangeably.)

Given enough encoded text, you can find those symbols that occur most frequently and map them to *e, t, a, o,* and right on down the line.

Something similar holds true for all languages that are written using a phonetic alphabet. In each language some letters will be common and some will not. In English, *e* and *t* are common; *q* and *z* are not. In Hebrew, *yud* and *vav* are common; *gimmel* and *zayin* are not. Each language has its own table of letter frequencies that can be used to identify *normal* text in that language.

I emphasized the word "normal" in the last paragraph for a good reason.

It is perfectly possible to write a large text that doesn't obey the letter-frequency tables. Ernest Vincent Wright wrote a whole novel in English, *Gadsby*, without using the letter *e* once. The German poet Gottlob Burmann wrote some 130 poems in his career, never once using the letter *r*. He even learned to exclude the letter from his ordinary speech!

But these exceptions prove the main point. In the *normal* usage of a language, letters are used with frequencies characteristic of that language. The works mentioned above were *intentionally* different. The authors went to some effort to exclude a particular letter. That exclusion forms a pattern that we can measure objectively by counting the frequencies of letters.

Of course, the frequency of letters in any given text won't conform rigidly to the frequency tables. Like the coin-flipping and dice-rolling experiments we talked about in chapter 6, there'll be some variation — a spread.

We know how to compute this spread for random processes like coin flipping or dice rolling. The formula is given in equation (A8) of Appendix A on my Web site. For our purposes, we're going to use the same formula for estimating the spread in the frequencies of symbols in meaningful text.

Please note that this spread is an approximation. It's not perfect, but we'll see that it works very well in practice.

Could a Monkey Write The Cat in the Hat?

Is it remotely possible that a monkey on a typewriter could dash out *The Cat in the Hat?*

Not a chance.

Let's prove that right now, using the ideas we just discussed, along with the chi-squared test from chapter 6. We're going to be very generous. We won't require our monkey to type punctuation, spaces, or capital letters.

We'll assume only that the monkey is equally likely to type any of the 26 letters of the English alphabet. This is a lot like our study of the digits of π in chapter 6. In this case we have 26 letters to count. Therefore, we have 25 degrees of freedom, since we really only need to keep tabs on any 25 of the letters in order to get a full accounting for all 26.

Now, it's impossible to have an infinite number of monkeys here on earth. Let's estimate how many monkeys we could cram in. The earth has about 200 million square miles of area, counting oceans, deserts, mountains, and ice fields. That works out to about 5 million billion square feet. By building skyscrapers we might conceivably cram in as many as 200 monkeys per square foot of surface, housing at most a billion billion monkeys. We'll guess that by typing very quickly a monkey could type one new manuscript every second. We'll also be ridiculous and say that all those monkeys have been typing away furiously since the Big Bang, which astronomers tell us was less than a billion billion seconds ago.

So, at most, we have a slush pile with a billion billion billion billion manuscripts waiting to be read. Carl Sagan would have loved it! Let's compute the odds that one of those manuscripts contains *The Cat in the Hat*.

We'll use the software discussed in "A Final Note" at the back of this book to solve this problem. I typed in the full text of *The Cat in the Hat* on my computer in order to run the chi-squared test on it. Unfortunately, I can't make this text publicly available since it's copyrighted. If you want to check my work, you'll have to type it yourself.

The results are as follows.

The text has 5,247 letters. If a monkey were typing that many letters randomly, then we'd expect each letter to show up about 219 times, plus or minus 14.5. (For the math on this, see Appendix A.) But in *The Cat in the Hat*, the letter t appears 618 times! So t has a Z-score of more than 27, all by itself. The letter j appears only 2 times; q and z don't appear at all. All three get Z-scores of about -15. The rest of the letters fall somewhere in between. Most of them also have large Z-scores.

The chi-squared value turns out to be about 3,970. For a text typed by a monkey, we'd expect a chi-squared of about 25. The probability that a monkey could create a text with a chi-squared value of 3,970 is impossibly small. Imagine poor Professor Sagan saying, "one chance in billions of billions of billions…" for hours and hours. But our monkeys don't have that much luck. Even if there were billions of billions of other galaxies, each with billions of billions of planets, each equipped with an army of monkeys like ours, that's still not enough monkeys to bring such a result within the realm of even remote possibility.

This is proof positive that *The Cat in the Hat* could not be produced by a monkey mashing keys at random on a typewriter.

Please notice an interesting fact here. We could have proved this fact without knowing a word of English. All we needed was a computer-readable copy of the text and a list of the letters that made up the text. The software that runs the chi-squared test did the rest.

We'll see in future chapters that the same holds true of the Bible code. We'll be able to run our tests without knowing Hebrew. But more of that when we have a few more tools.

Now we can get back to the main question: how to get the computer to help our worn-out intern read through the monkeys' slush pile.

AUTOMATING THE SLUSH PILE

We have just seen how software can compare a set of letter frequencies to our expectations for a random distribution. But why should we compare only to a random distribution?

We know how frequently each letter of our alphabet occurs in English text. (We can either look it up from published tables, or we can program a computer to read through a sample of English text and compute the frequencies of all the letters.) We can also estimate the spread in each of these letters.

This is a little different from the cases we've studied before. In our coin-flipping experiments, we assumed that heads and tails were equally likely and that the spread for heads and tails was the same. Likewise, in our dice experiments and our study of the digits of π, we assumed that all digits were equally likely and that each would have the same spread. The same principle held true in our study of monkey typing in this chapter.

Now, however, we are saying that *e* will occur about 13 percent of the time, *t* 10 percent of the time, and so on down to the most infrequent letters, *q* and *z*. So now the spreads for each letter will also be different.

But the principle of the chi-squared test is the same.

For each letter we can still compute an expected frequency and a spread, and that's all we need in order to compute a Z-score.

Suppose someone gives us a text sample written in German. The frequencies of the various letters in German are quite different than they are in English. We can have our computer calculate the actual frequencies of letters in our text. For each letter, we can compare the observed frequency to the expected frequency, getting a Z-score for that letter. Finally we can sum up the squares of the Z-scores for all the letters to get the chi-squared value for the text. In this way we could prove that the sample German text is not English, even if we don't speak either language.

The mathematical details for all this are found in Appendix B on my Web site. It doesn't matter whether you follow every single detail here. The important thing to understand is that every language has its own characteristic frequencies for each letter. If you have a table of these characteristic frequencies, you can use the chi-squared test to determine how likely it is that a text is written in that language.

WHEELS WITHIN WHEELS

There's more.

Code-breakers have known for a long time that you can also count the frequencies of pairs of letters in a text. The standard term for a letter pair is a "digram."

Some common digrams are "th" and "st." In fact, "th" is the most common digram in the English language, occurring about 37 times in every 1,000 digrams of normal English.

In the same way, we can define a trigram as a three-letter cluster. A common trigram in English is "the." Another is "ion."

We've already seen that each language has its own typical table of letter frequencies. Each language also has a table of digram and trigram frequencies. The tables for English are quite different from the tables for German or Latin.

Please note that these tables are big! English has 26 letters, which means it has 676 possible digrams and 17,576 possible trigrams. Without computers to keep track of these beasts, we'd be in big trouble. But with computers, it's all pretty simple.

The mathematics of chi-squared testing is really the same, whether you're looking at frequency tables of letters, digrams, or trigrams. In all three cases, we can program the computer to compute Z-scores for each letter frequency (or digram or trigram). Then we just have the machine add up the squares of all the Z-scores to give us a chi-squared value. It would be tremendously tedious for a human to do all that, but computers don't get bored.

And that's a good thing, because we're going to ask the computer to do a lot of hard work with these tables in the next few chapters. Let's remember our goal. We want to develop a test for the Bible code. Our test will tell us whether the ELSs embedded at various intervals in the text are *intentional* or *random*. We've learned in the last few chapters how to measure randomness for simple experiments with dice and coins. Our problem is that human language is not simple and it's not random. As we've seen in this chapter, letters, digrams, and trigrams occur with certain characteristic frequencies in each language.

The puzzle we have to solve is how to define what we mean by "random" ELSs in a nonrandom text.

Probably the simplest way to find the answer is to take a little detour into a topic that may seem irrelevant. It'll only last for two chapters, and it will turn out to be worthwhile in the end. Do you mind?

We're going to investigate, study, examine, research, explore, and probe the topic of redundancy.

8

Stamp Out and Eliminate Needless Redundancy

My friend Donald once launched a personal campaign to eliminate redundancy.

This was back in college, when people are often too idealistic for their own good. Anyway, for a while Donald got to be a tad bit difficult to talk to.

Listen in on this hypothetical conversation with Donald, and you'll see what I mean.

Several of us are sitting in the cafeteria and a cute girl comes through the line. I tilt my head in her direction. "Wow! She's got a really unique hairstyle!"

Donald stares down his nose at me in disdain. "*Really* unique?" he says, dragging out the word "really" in a way that only an Englishman could do correctly. Donald isn't English, so he sounds ridiculous, but he powers on anyway. "Since the word 'unique' means 'one of a kind,' perhaps you'd like to explain how anything could be more 'one of a kind' than 'one of a kind'? Or do you mean that some hairstyles are imaginarily unique, but in this particular case, the uniqueness is not imaginary but real. In which case — "

"Oh, shut up," I say, which is how Donald's friends concede defeat. By this time, the girl is gone, and none of us care.

I'm glad to say that Donald got his comeuppance. I'm even gladder to say that I was there to see it.

It happened in Statistics 301. Our college, in its infinite wisdom, had decided that the same class in statistics would do nicely for math majors, business majors, psychology majors, and social science majors. I was a math student, and Donald was a business major, so we wound up in the same class, which was taught by Professor Keith Anderson.

Dr. Anderson was one of the most honest men I've ever met. To him, honesty meant that you should speak as precisely as possible to avoid appearing to say something incorrect. He never called a box a "box." That wasn't accurate enough. It might be misinterpreted. So he called it a "rectangular parallelepiped."

Eventually our class got to the subject of probability. As I mentioned earlier in this book, mathematicians represent all probabilities by numbers between zero and one. Dr. Anderson liked to talk about probabilities, and a lot of his sentences began with the words, "There is a finite probability that…"

For example, "There is a finite probability that all the molecules of air in this room could bunch together in one corner, leaving you all gasping for breath."

What he meant was that the probability was some computable number greater than zero — that it was not infinitesimal. His use of "finite" in that phrase carried technical meaning and was not superfluous.

But Donald didn't know that, and pretty soon he got fed up with all this talk of finite probabilities. Finally one day he raised his hand. "Dr. Anderson, is there any such thing as an infinite probability?"

Dr. Anderson turned to look at him and shook his head. "No, Donald, all probabilities are between zero and one."

A huge smile spread across Donald's face. "Then why are you using the redundant phrase 'finite probability,' when there can't be any such thing as an infinite probability?"

At which point all of the math majors in the room hooted with laughter. "You moron!" one of them yelled. "Don't you know about infinitesimals?"

Donald, of course, did not.

Dr. Anderson gravely quieted the room. "Donald," he said, "a little knowledge can be a dangerous thing."

I'm happy to say that after this incident Donald's campaign against redundancy quieted down considerably.

Redundancy is a natural feature of any language, as we're going to discover in this chapter. This means that Donald's campaign was hopeless from the outset. Not only hopeless, but also counterproductive.

WHY REDUNDANCY IS GOOD

Actually, redundancy is helpful. I discovered this recently when I began teaching my children the Hebrew alphabet.

First, I explained that Hebrew is usually written using consonants only, without any vowels. Immediately my daughter Gracie wanted to know how you could read something without vowels.

I picked up a pen and started writing in English:

```
C_n y__ r__d th_s s_nt_nc_? _t _s
wr_tt_n w_th__t v_w_ls, b_t m_st
p__pl_ c_n r__d _t w_th n_
pr_bl_m.
```

Gracie picked her way through the words triumphantly. "Hey, I can read it!" she said. Then she went running off to tell my wife that you don't need vowels.

And it's true. Vowels are almost always redundant (in the sense of exceeding what is necessary) in written communication if you know the language well. But don't they make life easier? Redundancy makes reading much easier, even for native speakers.

In the same way, redundancy helps us add subjective elements to our sentences. Objectively, "really unique" isn't any more descriptive than "unique." But subjectively, it adds emotional content, especially if you put a little oomph on the word "really."

English is redundant at many levels. The spoken language carries significantly more information than we really need for communication. This is valuable when you're talking with foreigners. If their pronunciation isn't the best, you can still understand them because the spoken language carries so much extra information. Similarly, when you're talking on a bad phone line, the natural redundancies in English make it possible for you to understand what you're hearing.

So redundancy is good, because it allows you to remove part of a message without losing *any* of the meaning. It enables us to correct distortions and errors in our communication.

The problem is that redundancy is expensive. If you're talking on the phone long-distance, a little redundancy will make sure that your message gets across. But a lot of redundancy will mean that you wind up paying more than you should. So there's a trade-off. You want a little redundancy but no more than necessary.

Because of this trade-off, the communications industry has spent many years and lots of money to study redundancy. The really big breakthrough in the subject came in 1948, when Claude Shannon founded the science of information theory. The central concept Shannon used was the notion of entropy.

ALL ABOUT ENTROPY

Entropy is an idea used by physicists to measure disorder. It's been much discussed in the popular press because of its implications in the creation-evolution debate. We won't get into that here, because it's off the subject. I mention it only to say this: The entropy defined in information theory is slightly different from the entropy of thermodynamics, at least on the surface. Mathematically, there is a deep and beautiful connection. We won't explore that connection here because the mathematics is fairly difficult.

In information theory, engineers face the following problem. Suppose we have a message to be sent over a digital communication line. (When we say digital, we mean that we'll encode the message as a sequence of 0s and 1s.) The problem is that there is an infinite number of ways to encode the message! How shall we encode our message most cheaply?

Obviously, the cheapest encoding is the one that uses the fewest 0s and 1s. That is, the cheapest encoding has the least redundancy.

Now engineers don't think in terms of redundancy. Instead, they define a quantity called "entropy," which is effectively the opposite of redundancy. A message with the least possible redundancy has the highest possible entropy.

So the cheapest encoding will have what engineers call "maximal entropy," and there's a formula to compute what that maximal entropy is. But it gets better (at least if you're an engineer). There's also a simple scheme for encoding a message to achieve maximal entropy. The scheme is called "Huffman encoding," if you're interested. It's the basic idea behind all those compression programs people use on computers to save file space. This is another fascinating topic that's off-subject, so we'll say no more on it.

We're going to use the notion of entropy in our investigation of the Bible code. Here's why.

One way to think of entropy is as a measure of randomness. A message with high entropy looks very random, very disordered (like a string of letters randomly joined together). Low entropy, however, means lots of order. We see meaningful arrangements and patterns, such as our language's commonly used digrams and trigrams, and right on up through understandable words, phrases, and sentences. There's lots of redundancy in the sense of an abundance of "unnecessary" information, like the written vowels we focused on earlier.

So a high degree of redundancy and order in a text will result in a measurement of low entropy. A high degree of randomness, on the other hand, will result in a measurement of high entropy.

The idea of entropy provided the trigger for this book. Consider the following statement from an eighteenth-century rabbi, Eliyahu ben Shlomo, better known as "the Vilna Gaon," remembered in Jewish circles as one of the greatest sages ever: "All that was, is, and will be unto the end of time is included in the Torah, the first five books of the Bible."

There's a full discussion of this quote on page 2 of Jeffrey Satinover's *Cracking the Bible Code*. The sage's comment provides a deep philosophical basis for the Bible code and carries widespread approval among Bible-coders. Satinover continues quoting Rabbi Eliyahu as he expands on this statement: "…and not merely in a general sense, but including the details of every person individually, and the most intimate details of everything that ever happened to him from the day of his birth until his death; likewise of every kind of animal and beast and living thing that exists, and of herbage, and of all that grows or is inert."

Now before you dismiss this as rabbinical hyperbole, let me say that mathematically it's all quite possible. It would take superhuman intelligence to encode all those details, but it could be done, in principle. We're not here to examine possibilities, though; we're here to find out if the claim is correct.

Entropy provides us a powerful tool for testing this claim. If we calculate a low degree of entropy in a text, it's an indication of order, a sign of meaningful information. The more meaningful information, the lower the entropy. If the Torah contains so much information embedded as ELSs in the text, then the entropy of these ELSs in the Torah must be lower than we would ordinarily expect. I'll spend some time explaining exactly what this means, but there is no way around this fact.

Let me repeat this for emphasis. If you encode enormous quantities of meaningful information in the Torah, then the entropy of the Torah's ELSs must be low. Entropy thus becomes one of the valuable tools for determining the Bible code's validity.

HOW TO MEASURE ENTROPY

Every silver lining has a cloud, of course. Entropy is a powerful tool, but it can be defined only by a mathematical formula. I've promised to keep the math out of the main body of this book. If you want to see the formula, check out equation (C1) in Appendix C on my Web site. If you're a techhead, you might want to browse through Appendix C right now, because there are some very entertaining things to know about entropy. If you're not into that, here are the two main facts you need to know.

1. To compute the entropy of a text, we have to compute the probability tables for letters (or digrams or trigrams), as we discussed in chapter 7.

2. A totally random text has maximal entropy.

TESTING ENTROPY ON REAL TEXTS

Fine. Entropy is a magic formula that will solve all our problems (except possibly world hunger). Let's try it out!

For starters, we'll look at the digits of π. Now the digits of π are supposed to be patternless, unpredictable. Random. Let's test that.

We'll run my entropy analysis software on the digits of π, computing three different probability tables: the table for single digits, the table for digrams, and the table for trigrams. We talked about these tables in chapter 7. There, we were interested in doing chi-squared analyses. We'll use the *same* probability tables in this chapter for studying entropy. As a reminder, if you want to do these calculations on your own computer, you can get the software for free at my Web site. See "A Final Note" at the back of this book for directions.

In Table 8.1, I've summarized the results of my computer calculations for the entropy of a text containing the first 49,981 digits of π:

Maximal Entropy	3.321928
Digit Entropy	3.321842
Digram Entropy	3.321282
Trigram Entropy	3.317162

TABLE 8.1: ENTROPY MEASUREMENTS OF THE FIRST 49,981 DIGITS OF π

The "maximal entropy" is the largest entropy possible for a text composed of ten different characters — in this case, the digits 0 through 9. See the discussion around equation (C4) in Appendix C on my Web site for more details on this. You would see this maximal entropy only if all the characters occurred with equal probability. If you look at an infinite number of digits of π, you'll see that they do occur with equal probability.

However, if you only look at a finite number of digits, you'll find some spread in the probabilities. Therefore, the entropy you measure will be slightly less than the maximal entropy. That's what we see in Table 8.1. The entropies we compute from each of our three different probability tables are practically the same.

If you read Appendix C very closely, you'll find a satisfactory reason why the entropies computed using digrams and trigrams are slightly less than for single digits. It has to do with the finite size of the text we're using — "only" about 50,000 digits. If we used a text with a million digits, the discrepancy would be much smaller.

But overall, the results are excellent! We see that π has an entropy very close to the maximal value, and we understand why there's a small discrepancy. The results are much the same for single digits, digrams, and trigrams.

Very well. The digits of π have very close to the maximal entropy. That's reasonable, because those digits are very disordered — they're random.

Now let's try the same thing for *The Cat in the Hat*. Remember that this text is not random, so we don't expect to find the maximal entropy. This text carries meaningful patterns in it — words, phrases, sentences. We expect to find an entropy less than the maximal value.

An interesting fact: With this text, we're working with 26 letters instead of 10 digits. You can stir up a bigger mess with 26 letters than you can with 10 digits, so the maximal entropy is higher in this case.

Table 8.2 shows the results of running the entropy calculations.

Maximal Entropy	4.700439
Letter Entropy	4.075011
Digram Entropy	3.619525
Trigram Entropy	3.088436

TABLE 8.2: ENTROPY MEASUREMENTS OF THE CAT IN THE HAT

The "maximal entropy" here — about 4.7 — is the largest entropy possible for a text with 26 characters.

The actual entropy of *The Cat in the Hat,* based on the letter tables, is about 4.07, considerably less than the maximal entropy. We expected that. No surprises here.

But wait a minute! Look at the digram and trigram entropies!

What kind of tomfoolery is this? We've just measured the entropy of *The Cat in the Hat* three different ways, but we received three quite different answers depending on whether we used the table for single letters, digrams, or trigrams. Shouldn't there be a single value of entropy for the text?

What's going on here? Can we blame these wide differences on the finite size of our text? After all, it contains only 5,247 letters. Is that the problem?

The answer is no. Although the text is awfully short, my software computes the effect this ought to have on the measured entropy. That explains part of the shortfall, but there's still a huge discrepancy.

The fact remains: Something strange is going on here. Why do we get three answers so different? Is this all meaningless hocus-pocus?

As Dr. Anderson would have said, a little knowledge is a dangerous thing. Fact is, I haven't told you the whole story yet. Our statistical analysis of language has an extra facet we haven't explored yet, because I didn't want to make this chapter too long.

There's a simple explanation, and we'll get to it next. The answer will play a key role in helping us to unlock the mystery of the Bible code.

9

"LIES, D-LIES, AND STATISTICS"

Professor Keith Anderson (the same one who humbled my friend Donald) always told the truth, the whole truth, and nothing but the truth. One day that caused him a serious problem.

Dr. Anderson was a deeply spiritual man. I never heard him say a word that came within a mile of being a cussword. He never said "golly," "gee," or "doggone." Then our statistics class reached Section 3-5, "The Art of Statistical Deception." There in our textbook, a well-known quote by Benjamin Disraeli confronted us: "There are three kinds of lies: lies, d**ned lies, and statistics."

Dr. Anderson could not simply pass over this quote. It made an important point, one we needed to hear. On the other hand, he wasn't going to say That Word. What to do? Smirks ran around the classroom while we waited for the lecture to begin. Silence hung in the air so thick that the good professor had no need to rap on his desk with a pointer to get our attention.

"There are three kinds of lies," Dr. Anderson began, looking around the room calmly. "Lies…D-lies, and statistics."

The class erupted in guffaws. Steve, sitting next to me, leaned over, winked broadly, and asked me, "What's a D-lie?"

"I think it's a hydroelectric lie," I said, thinking I was clever.

We had a field day with Dr. Anderson's squeamishness. If I ran into Steve today, I'm sure he'd remember. But I think our professor had the last laugh, because his lecture was unforgettable. What we learned that day has stuck with me for a long time.

We learned how you can manipulate statistics to say just about anything you jolly well please. It's actually pretty easy, once you know how. I hear statistical lies in many a politician's speech. Journalists often are no better. For sheer nonsense value, sportscasters can be the biggest offenders of all.

It's remarkable that I learned so much about lying from a man who only told the truth. Wherever you are, Dr. Anderson, I salute your integrity.

A SHORT COURSE IN LYING

Statistics can make lying easy.

Want a ridiculous example?

About half the people in your city are male; about half are female. Therefore, the "average" person in your city is a half-male/half-female gender blender!

Nobody actually makes this particular mistake, of course, because the result is absurd. But I've heard people reach logical-sounding conclusions using reasoning just as silly.

Suppose everybody in your company gets a pay cut. Everybody, that is, except the company president, who decides to double his own salary. Wouldn't you be delighted to read in the annual report that the "average" salary of employees rose 10 percent?

Don't laugh. Statistics like this show up in the business section of your newspaper every week.

The lesson here is that statistics are useless unless they're interpreted correctly. In chapter 8, we ran headfirst into inconsistencies in our entropy findings for *The Cat in the Hat*. Could it be that we haven't interpreted our findings correctly?

LIFE, DEATH, AND ENTROPY

Entropy is a statistical measure of disorder. In chapter 8, we measured the entropy of the digits of π in three different ways, and we got pretty much the same result each time. Then we tried the same thing on *The Cat in the Hat* and got three quite different answers.

How can there be three different entropies for the same text? Which is the "right" one? Or are they all wrong?

To answer these questions, let's back up a step. Recall that entropy can be thought of as the opposite of redundancy. A low entropy means a high level of redundancy, reflecting an abundance of meaningful patterns of information.

Redundancy means that you can remove some part of the message without losing any information.

Let's try an example. Imagine you're locked away in a Third-World prison, accused of a crime you didn't commit. Speaking through an interpreter, your sadistic guard forces you to play a deadly game.

"I will choose a letter at random from one of your depraved books, filthy American! If you guess the letter correctly, you will live! If not, then we will shoot you at once."

The guard goes into the next room, and you hear the sound of pages turning. "I have made my choice, American! Now guess!"

You sit there in your chair, sweating. The most common English letter is *e,* which makes up about 13 percent of any text. Wonderful. You have at best a 13 percent chance of survival.

"Give me a clue," you say in your most pathetic voice. "I've got children at home."

"How many children, American?"

"Ten," you say, hoping he believes you.

By a miracle, he does. "Very well, foreign devil! I will give you ten clues."

Now what sort of clue can you ask for? Finally you say, "What letter comes just before the chosen letter?"

The guard consults the book. "It is an *a.*"

That doesn't tell you much. "What letter comes before that?" you ask.

"*H,*" says the guard.

Your mind spins furiously. *Ha_*. The third letter could be *d* or *m* or *s* or…anything. No, not quite anything. It probably isn't an *a,* an *e,* or an *o.* So you've made progress. You ask again. "What letter comes before that?"

"*E,*" says the guard. "Are you not yet ready to guess, running dog?"

Of course you aren't. You ask for more letters, and the guard supplies them. As he does, a guess forms in your mind. Soon you know it with a certainty. To play it safe, you ask for all ten letters. Finally the guard gives the last one.

You replay the letters again in your mind, just to make sure. *Catintheha_.* Yes! You lean back in your chair and take a deep breath. "The letter you chose is *t!*"

The guard walks back into the room, his face sagging with disappointment. "Correct, filthy American. You are lucky this day, are you not?"

You gravely agree as he escorts you to freedom.

Do you see what's happened? As the guard supplied you with more letters, your information about the missing letter increased, due to the redundancy of the English language. By the time you had ten letters, you could be certain of the result.

With the first clue, you could exclude only a few possible letters. With each succeeding letter, you excluded a few more. At a certain point, you were certain. After that, the extra letters were really no help at all; they only confirmed what you already knew.

Resolving the Discrepancy

Now what does this have to do with the apparent contradictions in our entropy findings for *The Cat in the Hat?*

The answer is simple. When you have the table of letter probabilities, you know only a little about the English language. You know that *e* is the most common letter, that *t* is the next most, and so on. So your ability to guess a randomly chosen letter is limited.

When you have the digram frequencies, you know a bit more. If I ask you what letter is likely to come after *t,* you can consult the digram table and find that *h* is an excellent answer, while *n* is not.

Here's another example. I'm thinking of a word starting with *q.* What's the second letter?

If you answered anything but *u,* English isn't your native language.

U isn't the most common letter in the language, but it's almost always the letter that follows *q*.

With the trigram frequencies, you know more yet. If I ask what letter is likely to come after *th*, you'll find that *e* is the best answer, but *t* is one of the worst.

In a sense, redundancy is a relative thing. The clues your guard gave made his chosen letter redundant to you but not to him. He lacked your knowledge of English. Redundancy depends on knowledge.

Knowing the digram table increases the redundancy of the text. Knowing the trigram table increases the redundancy even more.

This explains the discrepancies we saw earlier. The information in the digram table increases the redundancy of *The Cat in the Hat* and therefore reduces the entropy. The information in the trigram table reduces the entropy even more.

So what is this thing called entropy, really?

Our calculation of entropy reflects the amount of new information provided by each letter in the text. A native English speaker has a deep intuition about the language. If I show you a thousand letters of English text, the odds are excellent that you can guess the next letter. If I show you only two letters, you'll have a much harder time. If I show you one letter, you'll have a very hard time. And if I show you no letters, forcing you to guess, you'll do quite poorly.

This is why we got different values of entropy when using letter frequencies, digram frequencies, and trigram frequencies. By increasing our knowledge, we reduced the entropy.

The inconsistency in our entropy findings for *The Cat in the Hat* was no real inconsistency at all. We simply didn't understand that entropy is relative to knowledge. The more knowledge we have, the lower the entropy we'll compute.

What about the digits of π? Why didn't extra knowledge reduce the entropy of π?

Before we answer, suppose that I show you a thousand digits of π. Can you guess the next one?

Of course not, unless you're one of those weird people who've memorized thousands of digits of π. Even then, I could break your luck by skipping the first couple of billion digits and showing you a fresh batch that you hadn't memorized.

It doesn't matter whether I show you a thousand digits of π or two or one or none. If I ask you to guess the next digit, your odds are one in ten of getting it right. The digits of π are random. They have no redundancy at all. π has the maximum entropy possible for a text made up of ten digits.

That's why our computation of the entropy for π was essentially the same when we used the digit frequencies or the digrams or the trigrams. The digram table and the trigram table added no new knowledge.

Long-Range Disorder

Very well, then. We've seen that nearby letters provide information about a missing letter. What about letters far away?

For example, suppose you're back in prison with your friendly guard, and he wants to play the game again. You beg for ten clues, and he agrees. But this time he counts backward *a thousand letters*. "Filthy American, I find an *s* exactly one thousand letters before the chosen letter! Are you ready to guess?"

You're terrified now. "Give me another clue, please!"

He counts backward another thousand letters. "This time, I find an *n!*"

It's hopeless. The clues he's giving you are worthless, no matter how good your skills in English. In despair, you say, "I'll guess that the chosen letter is *e!*"

"Wrong, foreign devil! Allow me to introduce you to your jury: Mr. Smith and Mr. Wesson!"

What's gone wrong?

Natural language has an order to it, but only over short distances. The digram table tells you which pairs of letters are likely to lie next to each other in English. The trigram table tells which trios of letters adjoin each other. But there is no table in the world that tells which letters are likely to lie exactly a thousand letters apart in a text.

English has short-range order but long-range disorder. These two facts are just as true in Hebrew as in English. And that's the key to unlocking the mystery of the Bible code. In the next chapter, we'll put all this together into a plan for cracking the code. We'll find a way to harness statistics to get at the truth.

I think Professor Anderson would be proud.

10

How to Crack the Bible Code

What I love about old people is that they always tell you exactly what they think.

What I hate about old people is that they always tell you exactly what they think.

When I was in graduate school, my wife, Eunice, and I had a friend at our church named Pearl who was about eighty years old. Pearl had sharp wits and a sharper tongue, and she had no hesitation about telling you anything. *Anything.*

One summer Eunice and I went out of town for a month or so. When we got back, Pearl came over to talk to us after church.

"Well, I had a radical," she began without prologue.

I stared at her blankly. *Radical? Radical what?* Then it hit me. A radical mastectomy. Obviously, this was going to be girl-talk. I half-turned and began looking around to see how I could discreetly ease my way out of this conversation.

But Pearl wasn't about to let half of her audience escape. "They gave me a wonderful prosthesis," she said.

With a colossal effort I kept a straight face. "That's...um, great." Meanwhile, my eyes were frantically scanning the room for an excuse, *any* excuse, to bail out.

"Here, I'll show you," Pearl said. Her hand shot out and latched on to mine. Before I could react, she yanked my hand up and clamped it firmly on the left side of her chest. "Squeeze that!" she ordered.

I knew Pearl. She wasn't going to let go of my hand without a struggle. I could either fight her or do as she said.

So I squeezed.

Pearl grinned and let go of my hand. "Feels like the real thing, don't it?"

I could feel my ears turning jalapeño hot. "Um…yeah!" I jammed both hands into the safety of my pockets.

Then all three of us collapsed in laughter.

The whole episode gave me a roaring case of cognitive dissonance. That prosthesis felt exactly like the real thing. I'm sure it made Pearl's year to have me squeeze it, but it was very disorienting to me. My head told me it was fake, but my fingers told a very different story. Was it real? I have no way (and no wish) to…ahem…repeat the experiment to find out.

In a way we have the same problem with the Great Rabbis Experiment. If Doron Witztum, Eliyahu Rips, and Yoav Rosenberg conducted their experiment exactly as they claim, then their results are quite impressive — the real thing, so to speak.

But as we discussed in chapter 4, we have strong reasons to think that they accidentally biased their experiment. The Great Rabbis Experiment appears flawed from the outset. That's why we've spent the last several chapters developing some new ideas. Now we're ready to tackle one of our two main questions.

Is the Bible code the real thing, or isn't it?

We now have enough tools to answer that question. In this chapter we'll map out a strategy for using those tools, then we'll apply the strategy first of all to test *The Cat in the Hat* for a "Bible code."

Meanwhile let's recap the main issue. Those who believe in the Bible code claim that meaningful information is encoded in the text of the Hebrew Bible as Equidistant Letter Sequences — ELSs. Skeptics insist that any such ELSs are due to random chance.

Fortunately, both of these claims have measurable consequences.

WHAT IF THE BELIEVERS ARE RIGHT?

If the believers are right, then we can imagine the following experiment. Take any text and choose some interval for skips, say 2 or 10 or 5,000. The interval doesn't matter for this experiment.

We'll now construct a "skip-text" as follows. Write out the text in lines the same length as the interval of skips. Then just read vertically down the columns, one after another.

As an example, if the text is *The Cat in the Hat* and the skip interval is 10, then the original text will look like this:

```
thesundidn
otshineitw
astoowetto
playsowesa
tinthehous
eallthatco
ldcoldwetd
ayisatther
ewithsally
wesatthere
```

...and so on.

The resulting "skip-text" will read like the following (as we now go *down* the columns of text reconstructed as above):

```
toaptelaewwahtoullneglwtw
klntubjewolecttolnasuedfs
mpeokaatlottiadamusyhagth
nldhtseoshhsmedhcsiiapsns...
```

Notice that the skip-text has some real English words in it: "to," "Jew," "lot," "dam," "hag," etc. It also has some English words spelled backwards: "let," "thaw," "low," etc. These forward and backward words represent the ELSs in the original text with a skip of 10.

For *The Cat in the Hat,* we expect that all such ELSs are random. For the Bible, everybody agrees that at least some of the ELSs are also random. The skeptics say that they are all random. The believers claim that some are not random — they were put there intentionally.

Now if the believers are right, then an author intentionally placed some ELSs in the Bible, and *that author intended for us to find them.* (It makes no sense to send a message unless you intend it to be detected.) To detect intentional ELSs in the text, we must show that the ELSs we see are different in some way from those we'd expect by random chance. This doesn't necessarily mean *more* ELSs. It could just mean more of some ELSs and fewer of others.

If the believers are right, then the ELSs in each skip-text taken from the Bible will be measurably different from those you'd predict in a random text.

Let's define what we mean by a random text, because this is crucial. We mean a text with exactly the same letter frequencies as the original but scrambled using some random process. For example, snip out all the letters of the original text and put them in a hat. Then shake the hat, draw out letters one by one, and paste them down in order to create a new text. This new random text will have exactly the same frequencies of each letter as the original did. But the digram and trigram frequencies will be different — they'll be random. They won't reveal the kind of language structure we talked about in chapter 9.

Appendix D on my Web site explains how to compute the digram and trigram frequencies you'd expect to see in a random text. That appendix also describes the exact method we'll use to produce our random texts. Note that if a text is random, its skip-texts are also random. For technical reasons explained in the appendix, when we talk about random texts from here on, we'll actually mean a skip-text constructed from a random text.

In chapter 8 we noted Rabbi Eliyahu ben Shlomo's statement that every detail of every person's life is found in the Torah. Bible-coders interpret this to mean that many of these details must be encoded as ELSs. If their interpretation is correct, the Torah must be chock-full of ELSs at many different skips. No matter which skip we consider, we ought to see many more meaningful ELSs than random chance predicts. This means that every skip-text must contain many more meaningful words (spelled both backward and forward) than you'd expect to see in a random text.

Now these extra words are not just random conglomerations of letters. They are real words (or dates, in the case of the Great Rabbis Experiment). Real words have characteristic digram and trigram frequencies. So do dates.

The digram and trigram frequencies of intentionally encoded words are different from those you'd expect by random chance, and they result in different digram and trigram entropies than those you'd get by random chance.

Using skip-texts, we can measure these entropies. If the believers are right, then we should see a statistically significant difference. That is, we should see a difference that could happen by chance only once in billions of billions of billions…of times.

WHAT IF THE SKEPTICS ARE RIGHT?

If the skeptics are right, then we can expect that the skip-texts taken from the original text will have the same distribution of words, on average, as those from a random text.

Actually, we need to refine that statement a bit.

We know that languages have short-range order. For example, in *The Cat in the Hat* we find these two commonly recurring phrases:

1. "said the Cat"
2. "the Cat in the Hat"

The first of these has the word "sit" encoded in it at a skip of two. The second has the word "tea" encoded twice at a skip of two. We're going to see lots of "sit" and "tea" ELSs at a skip of two — more than we'd expect in a random text. If we go to a skip of three, there are bound to be other ELSs that occur in other frequently occurring phrases. Again, we'll see more than would be normal for a random text.

If we look for ELSs at a skip of 200, we don't expect to see this effect, because there aren't any repeated phrases that are hundreds of characters long.

So we expect to see some "nonrandom" ELSs at short skips. As we examine longer and longer skips, eventually all the nonrandom ELSs should disappear. This is another aspect of our language's long-range "disorder" that we discussed in chapter 9.

Now we can restate what we expect to see.

If the skeptics are right, we expect that skip-texts taken from the original will have the same distribution of words, on average, as random skip-texts, *provided the skip is large enough.*

Now what do those weasel words "large enough" mean?

They mean that there is some threshold skip-value. We don't know exactly what that threshold will be; for now we'll guess that it's somewhere between 10 and 50. For skips larger than that threshold, we expect the original text to be indistinguishable from random text.

FOUR NATURAL TESTS FOR RANDOMNESS

One question remains: How will we compare a given skip-text taken from the original to a random skip-text?

We can use four tests:

1. Measure the digram entropy.
2. Measure the trigram entropy.
3. Do a chi-squared test of digram probabilities.
4. Do a chi-squared test of trigram probabilities.

These tests meet the first three requirements we stated in chapter 5. The measurements are natural (that is, they are measurements commonly used by scientists), they have no wiggle room, and they can distinguish between random text and nonrandom text that contains intentional messages. In the next few chapters, we'll use these tests on some nonbiblical texts, then make predictions about what we should see in the Bible.

DIGRAM ENTROPY CALCULATIONS
IN THE CAT IN THE HAT

All right, let's get started. We're going to run our first tests on *The Cat in the Hat.* If you remember how we defined a skip-text, you'll see that by taking a skip of 1, we just get back the original text.

The software I wrote for this book lets us automate the whole process of computing the entropy for the skip-texts at a large number of skips both for an original text and for randomized texts. We'll compute these for comparison purposes since our goal is to check whether the entropy of skip-texts taken from the original is different from what you'd see by random chance.

Let's do the random text computation first. We'll compute the digram entropy for 150 different randomized skip-texts, from a skip of 1 to a skip of 150. (As per our definition for "random" text, each of these 150 texts has the same letter frequencies as the original text in *The Cat in the Hat,* but the letters have been scrambled in a random order.) When we run the software, we find an average entropy of 4.0395 with a spread of 0.0022. (See Appendix C on my Web site for exact details on how the software computes these numbers.)

Next, let's run the software and compute the digram entropy of the original text of *The Cat in the Hat.* The result is 3.6195, which is quite a bit less than the average entropy for a random text. This lower entropy score indicates, as we would expect, that the original text of *The Cat in the Hat* is much more meaningful and orderly than random arrangements of the same letters.

How significant is this difference? To answer that, let's compute the Z-score, which we discussed in chapter 6. The Z-score turns out to be a whopping -191! That's as remarkable as finding a person with an IQ higher than about 3,000.

Finally, let's run the software and compute the digram entropy of 150 different skip-texts taken from the original *The Cat in the Hat* text, ranging from a skip of 1 to a skip of 150. The results are shown in Figure 10.1. At the skip of 1 (which simply reads the text in its original letter-order),

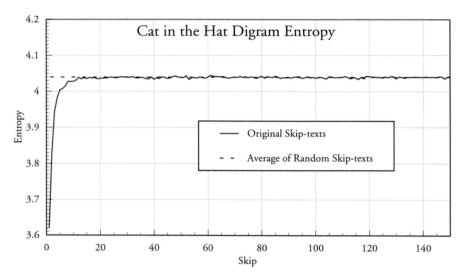

the entropy is 3.6195, as we found already. This shows up on the graph as the lower-left starting point for the solid black line. The numbers below the graph mark the 150 skip intervals we're measuring, while the numbers going up the graph's left side mark the levels of entropy.

For comparison, we'll also plot (on the horizontal dashed line) the average entropy of the 150 random skip-texts, which we calculated to be 4.0395.

Notice how quickly the entropy of *The Cat in the Hat* skip-texts comes into excellent agreement with the expected value for random texts. This is no great surprise. We guessed that skip-texts would be pretty close to random for skips larger than some threshold value.

It's helpful to zoom in on the plot to see just how good this agreement is. We'll do that in Figure 10.2, but this time, we'll show more information. We see again the solid black line indicating the entropy for the 150 skip-texts from *The Cat in the Hat.* We'll also plot the entropy for each of the 150 random skip-texts, shown by the gray line.

For additional perspective, we'll draw *three* horizontal lines. The middle line represents the average entropy for all random texts, the same level line shown in Figure 10.1. The top and bottom lines represent the average

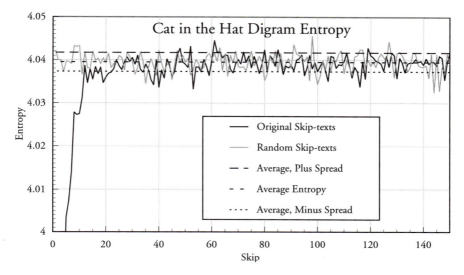

FIGURE 10.2: MAGNIFIED PLOT OF DIGRAM ENTROPIES OF THE CAT IN THE HAT

entropy plus or minus the spread, which we found to be 0.0022. So most of the points we plot for both the original and the random texts should be within the top and bottom horizontal lines. We expect to see some points fall outside this range, but not very many.

As you can see, for large skips the agreement between the original *The Cat in the Hat* text and the random texts is absolutely excellent. For skips greater than about 20, the digram entropy for both kinds of text appears to be virtually the same.

TRIGRAM ENTROPY CALCULATIONS
IN THE CAT IN THE HAT

Now that we know how it's done, we can quickly repeat the whole process for trigram entropies. Remember that the trigram entropy of *The Cat in the Hat* is substantially different from the digram entropy. Even for random-ized text, the digram entropy will not agree with the trigram entropy. This is because of the finite size of the text. (The math for this is gory. See Appendix C on my Web site if you really want to understand it.)

When we compute the trigram entropy for 150 different randomized texts, we find an average entropy of 3.7394 with a spread of 0.0036.

The original text in *The Cat in the Hat* has a trigram entropy of 3.0884. Once again, this is very far from the entropy of random texts. The Z-score is -181, which is very large. So we see that we are measuring an enormous discrepancy between random text and real, meaningful text.

As we did for digrams, we'll compute the trigram entropy of 150 different skip-texts from *The Cat in the Hat* and 150 randomly ordered skip-texts. The results appear in Figure 10.3 below.

Once again, for skips greater than about 20, the entropy of *The Cat in the Hat* skip-texts is indistinguishable from that of the random texts. This is pretty much what we expected.

DIGRAM CHI-SQUARED CALCULATIONS IN THE CAT IN THE HAT

It's all too tempting to declare victory over the poor Cat and move on directly to the Hebrew Bible.

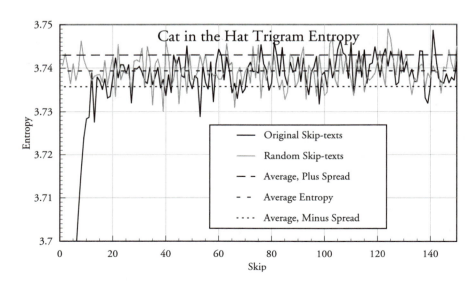

FIGURE 10.3: TRIGRAM ENTROPIES OF THE CAT IN THE HAT

Patience.

We're doing science here, and we need to accumulate all the data we can. It's always wise to be cautious, to check, double-check, and triple-check everything. What good will it do us to come to a quick answer unless we can prove beyond all doubt that it's the right answer?

So we're going to do a chi-squared test on the digrams of *The Cat in the Hat*.

First, let's recall what a chi-squared test does. Since we can measure the exact letter probabilities in the text, we can use the results of Appendix D (on my Web site) to compute the expected digram probabilities that we'd see in a random text. Also, we can compute the spread in those digram probabilities. We need both the expected probabilities and the spreads to do the chi-squared test. Once those are computed, the chi-squared test measures the total deviation of the observed digram probabilities from the expected probabilities. The higher the chi-squared value, the more deviation we're observing.

It's natural to see some variation in chi-squared analyses, and mathematicians have worked out how much deviation we ought to see on average.

That analysis and our exact calculation are spelled out on my Web site in Appendix B. As always, some subtle issues arise, and those are explained in Appendix D. For example, we include in the chi-squared analysis only those digrams that are expected to occur at least once. The English language has 26 letters in the alphabet, with 676 possible digrams. But some of these — such as "qx" — almost never occur. In a text the size of *The Cat in the Hat*, only 446 digrams are expected to appear more than once.

Now let's run the test.

First I set up the software to compute the chi-squared value of the digrams of 150 different randomized texts, measured at skips from 1 to 150. (Again, each of these random texts has the same letter frequencies as the original *The Cat in the Hat* text, but the letters are in scrambled order.) The results are no great surprise. The average chi-squared value was 351.9, with a spread of 25.6. These numbers are perfectly reasonable.

Then we run the test on 150 skip-texts of the original. The chi-squared value at skip 1 — for the text read in its original order — is 6948.2, which is absolutely enormous. The Z-score for this is about 258. Clearly, the original text is incredibly far from random — although we might have guessed that already!

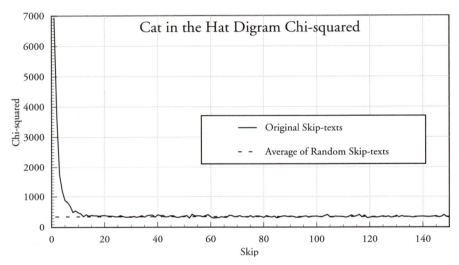

FIGURE 10.4: CHI-SQUARED ANALYSIS OF DIGRAMS IN THE CAT IN THE HAT

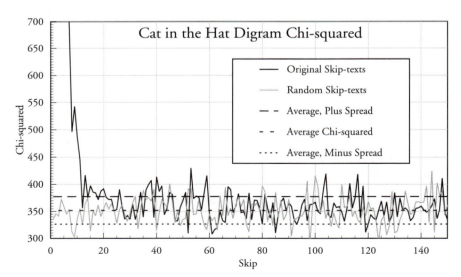

FIGURE 10.5: MAGNIFIED CHI-SQUARED ANALYSIS OF DIGRAMS IN THE CAT IN THE HAT

Now let's plot the results. Figure 10.4 shows the chi-squared values for the skip-texts taken from the original, plus a horizontal line representing the average value for the random texts.

Once again, we can't see much detail on this scale. We'll want to zoom in and look at the data more closely. The results are shown in Figure 10.5. We'll add a line that plots the chi-squared values for each of the 150 random skip-texts. And again we're showing three horizontal lines, representing the average for all random texts plus or minus the spread. As you can see, the plots don't stay strictly within those horizontal lines. We don't expect them to. But they're close. That's the normal behavior of random variables.

Again we see a threshold of about 20. For skips above that threshold, the chi-squared values are indistinguishable from a random text. This agrees nicely with our entropy calculations.

TRIGRAM CHI-SQUARED CALCULATIONS IN THE CAT IN THE HAT

We'll do one last run with our software. This time we'll study *The Cat in the Hat* using a chi-squared test of the trigrams.

The English language has 17,576 possible trigrams. Most of these don't appear in *The Cat in the Hat*. In fact, the program finds that only 1,340 trigrams are expected to occur more than once.

In the trigram test, we find the average chi-squared value for 150 randomized texts to be 1259.4 with a spread of 50.7. The original text of *The Cat in the Hat* has a chi-squared of 22,459. Wow! This is a Z-score of about 418. The trigrams tell the same story as the digrams — monkeys didn't type this text.

Now, in Figure 10.6, we'll plot the magnified chi-squared results for skip-texts from both the original and the random texts.

Just as before, all the skip-texts with skips above about 20 look as random as can be. The trigram chi-squared test shows no long-range order in *The Cat in the Hat*.

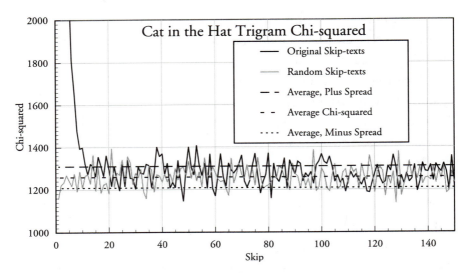

FIGURE 10.6: MAGNIFIED CHI-SQUARED ANALYSIS OF TRIGRAMS IN THE CAT IN THE HAT

WHAT HAVE WE PROVED?

Let's summarize what we've done in this chapter.

1. We've defined four tests of long-range order that can be run on any text.

2. We've run all four tests on *The Cat in the Hat.*

3. We've measured the point at which short-range order turns into long-range disorder. This happens at a skip of about 20, roughly where we expected.

You may be complaining that we haven't really proved anything here. Nobody expects to find a secret message from either God or Dr. Seuss in *The Cat in the Hat,* so why were we looking there? What's the point?

The point is that we're doing what scientists always do: We're calibrating our equipment. We're making predictions and verifying them. We're finding a few small surprises — such as the fact that trigram entropies differ quite a bit from digram entropies, even in fully random texts. We're getting a firm understanding of our tools and their limitations.

One limitation is obvious. For large skips, we're finding that the skip-texts look *pretty much* like random texts. But "pretty much" is *pretty vague.* Can't we do better? Can't we average out all those wiggles in our plots?

Yes, we can. In the next chapter, we'll show how to do this. And we'll find that we can refine our measurements almost without limit. We'll learn how to distinguish the real from the fake with astonishing precision.

It'll be...radical.

11

The Bible Code Under a Microscope

A lot can happen in a tenth of a second. You can blink an eye. You can read a word. You can get yourself killed.

I got engaged to a wonderful young lady on April Fool's Day during my second year of graduate school at Berkeley. The next day was a Friday. We chose that evening to break the news to our friends. Naturally, we all stayed out late talking. When we finished, we set out on foot for our apartments. Four of us were headed in the same direction.

Normally, we'd all have stayed in a tight cluster so we could keep an eye on Norma. Born with cerebral palsy, Norma had spent a good share of her life in institutions. Then, in her midthirties, she put together a bold sixteen-year plan to get her college diploma, taking one class per quarter. She faced tough odds. The cerebral palsy distorted her speech into a garbled smear of sound that took enormous patience to interpret. Her left hand had just enough coordination to type at about one word per minute. With her left arm locked at the elbow, clenching a joystick with thumb and one finger, she piloted her motorized wheelchair through the streets of Berkeley with all the grace of a giraffe on a unicycle. Norma had guts and she took no pity from anyone. I admired her immensely.

We took it as our duty to stay close to Norma, especially on the big streets.

The worst of these was Dwight Way — a one-way street, three lanes across, with a speed limit of forty miles per hour. The real limit, of course, was whatever the flow of traffic would bear, which was more like fifty-five.

Norma had to cross Dwight Way to get home, and we never let her cross it alone if we could help it. But this night we weren't paying attention. My fiancée and I were talking, wrapped up in our own little world and walking a bit slower than Norma's wheelchair. Another friend, Alice, walked along beside us, chattering about our impending leap into the jaws of matrimony.

Suddenly, the three of us realized that Norma had gotten ahead of our group. When she'd reached Dwight Way, she hadn't waited for us; she'd forged on ahead. Already she had navigated halfway across Dwight, and the pedestrian signal was blinking red.

I've crossed that street a thousand times, and it always blinks red exactly ten times before the signal changes, giving you plenty of time to get across the street. If you run, you can make it in three blinks. We didn't know how many red blinks we had left, but I guessed we had five or six.

My guess was dead wrong.

Like a pair of idiots, my lady and I began our dash across Dwight Way, my arm firmly around her shoulder. Don't ask how we thought we could help Norma. Really, there wasn't anything we could do.

Norma reached the curb just as the signal changed. We had crossed most of the middle lane. Lane three was empty.

At least it looked empty.

What I didn't see, until the last possible instant, was a car barreling down lane three. I'm sure the driver had been braking, but when the light turned green, he changed his mind and hit the gas.

My fiancée never saw it coming.

The next instant is a blurred eternity in my memory. The car appeared like a line drive out of nowhere. I somehow stopped in only two strides. The car flashed by, a foot in front of my face. Behind us, Alice screamed. Horns began honking.

And my lady?

Locked to my hip, her arm around my waist, my arm around her shoulder, Eunice stopped when I stopped — safe by inches.

I figure we missed the Reaper by a tenth of a second or so. For most purposes, that's a tiny interval of time. In our case, it was huge.

In this chapter we're going to see just how finely we can measure things in our Bible code tests. What we'll find is that we can split hairs quite accurately. We'll be able to measure things so finely that tiny differences will look huge.

The tool we'll use is called the Law of Large Numbers, which we first looked at in chapter 6. It's a very simple tool and very powerful. I won't guarantee that it'll save your life, but it will allow us to zoom in on the Bible code like a microscope.

THE LAW OF LARGE NUMBERS

Suppose you have a coin and you want to find out whether it's a fair coin. By definition, a fair coin has an equal probability of being flipped heads or tails. The probability of each is 0.5.

So you flip the coin 100 times, and you record the results. Let's say that you see 53 heads and 47 tails. Is the coin fair?

As we discussed in chapter 6, you expect to see 50 heads, with a spread of 5. So the theoretical probability is 0.5, and the spread in your probability measurements will be 0.05.

Right now, your experimental estimate of the probability of heads is 0.53. Your observed result differs from the expected value by less than one multiple of the spread. We compute a Z-score of 0.6. A statistician would say that you've observed a result that is "consistent with the hypothesis that the coin is fair."

But is the coin *really* fair? You still don't know for sure!

It should be obvious what to do next. Flip the coin another 100 times.

This time maybe you see 51 heads. So now you've seen 104 heads in 200 flips. Your best estimate of the probability of heads is 0.52.

Now here is the important point. The formula (A8) in Appendix A on my Web site tells us that your spread is now only about 0.035. Your new estimate is sharper than your old one.

Keep flipping the coin. As you do so, your estimate of the probability of heads will keep changing, and the spread will keep decreasing. *So your estimate will improve, the more data you take.*

If you take four times as much data, you'll cut the spread in half.

Take a hundred times as much data, and the spread reduces to a tenth of its original size.

We'll imagine that you're very patient and you've flipped the coin 10,000 times and you've seen 5,300 heads. Your estimate of the probability of heads is now 0.53, and the spread is only 0.005.

Is the coin fair?

Almost certainly not. The Z-score for your experiment is now 6, which is very large. Most of the time, in a truly random experiment, the Z-score will be less than 1. Rarely will it go over 3 by random chance. A Z-score of 6 is about as rare as an IQ of 196.

When you see a Z-score that high, it's a safe guess that the coin is not fair (or the person flipping it is cheating in some way).

How does all this apply to our experiments on the Bible code?

The Law of Large Numbers tells us that we can reduce the spreads by taking lots of data. In our case, that means analyzing lots of skip-texts both from the original and from randomized text.

In chapter 10 we ran four different experiments comparing original skip-texts to randomized texts, using 150 of each. This seemed to provide enough data to give quite precise results. For small skips, the original text was clearly very far from random. For large skips, it appeared to come into close agreement with the random texts, as we expected.

But how close? It's difficult to tell by eye. When we zoom in on the plots, we find two very wiggly lines. On average, they look about the same over a broad range of skips.

And that's the key.

If we calculate the average of many randomized texts, the wiggles will tend to average out and the spread will decrease.

Likewise, if we average the skip-text results from the original, the wiggles there will also average out. Here we have to be careful. For small skips, our results are very far from being random. But after a certain point, the results level out. What we need to do is average the results for all skips larger than some threshold value.

Then we can compare the two averages. Each of these measurements has a spread. Formula (A4) in Appendix A explains how to combine these two spreads into a composite spread. We can use that composite spread to determine a Z-score that tells us how far apart the two averages are.

THE CAT IN THE HAT COMES BACK

For fun, let's apply all this to *The Cat in the Hat*. But there's a question we have to answer first.

At what threshold skip-text shall we start averaging results?

Have a look at the figures in chapter 10 again. You'll see that the results for the original text start getting pretty close to the random results at a skip of about 10. However, "pretty close" still allows for a small discrepancy. You can still see some tiny differences out to skips of about 50. After that, both sets of results seem to fluctuate randomly with about the same amount of spread.

To be safe, then, for the skip-texts from the original we'll use a threshold of 50. That still leaves us with the original-text data from skip 50 to skip 150 to average over. With those 100 data points, the Law of Large Numbers ought to help out a lot. For the random texts, meanwhile, we'll use the results from all 150 skip-texts. The net effect is to reduce the effective spread to a tiny amount.

So we'll average the measurements for 100 skip-texts from the original text, and we'll average the measurements for 150 random skip-texts. Then we'll compare the two averages by computing a Z-score. This is a hefty calculation! But my software automates the entire process.

I've tabulated the results in Table 11.1.

Test	Original	Random Texts	Composite Spread	Z-score
Digram Entropy	4.039255	4.039523	2.86E-04	-0.936
Trigram Entropy	3.739385	3.739376	4.74E-04	0.019
Digram Chi-squared	356.5	351.9	3.326	1.383
Trigram Chi-squared	1275.8	1259.4	6.557	2.501

TABLE 11.1: Z-SCORES FOR COMBINED ANALYSES ON THE CAT IN THE HAT

As you can see, the Z-scores that we get when comparing the original text to randomized texts are pretty low. They're not exactly 0; we don't expect them to be. We expect them to be most often less than 2 and almost always less than 3.

And that's what we see.

THE REVISED STANDARD VERSION

Now we're ready to move on to a larger chunk of text. We'll take a big step closer to our ultimate target by analyzing an English translation of Genesis.

When the *Revised Standard Version* came out (the New Testament in 1946, the Old Testament in 1952), a lot of folks didn't like it. The language was too modern. The powerful rhythms of the *King James Version* had somehow gotten lost. And the new version didn't support certain doctrinal points as well as the old one had.

So far as I know, nobody has ever suggested that the RSV has a secret message from God hidden in it. More the opposite — some have hinted darkly that the RSV got a boost from Mr. Pitchfork.

As a test of our new and improved tools, let's have a look at the RSV text of Genesis. Our goal is to understand our tools better. In scientific language, we want to continue calibrating our software, to test its limits.

Every tool has limits, of course. No matter how good your microscope, it can only zoom so far. And cheap microscopes also split white light into colors like a prism.

In the same way, our software likely has some limits. We want to see how far we can push it. We want to see what kind of results we get in a noncoded text, before we go looking in the Hebrew Bible for the real thing.

I've done the calculations and plotted the results in Figures 11.2 through 11.5. You'll see that just as with *The Cat in the Hat,* we need to

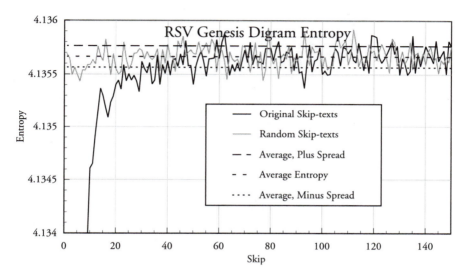

FIGURE 11.2: DIGRAM ENTROPIES OF THE RSV TEXT OF GENESIS

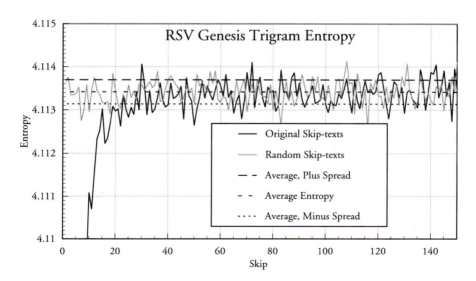

FIGURE 11.3: TRIGRAM ENTROPIES OF THE RSV TEXT OF GENESIS

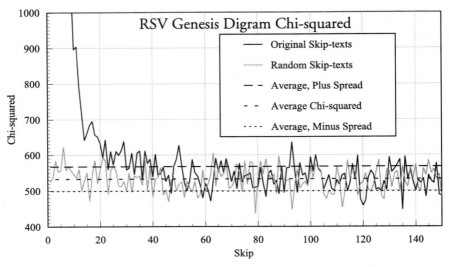

FIGURE 11.4: CHI-SQUARED ANALYSIS OF DIGRAMS IN THE RSV TEXT OF GENESIS

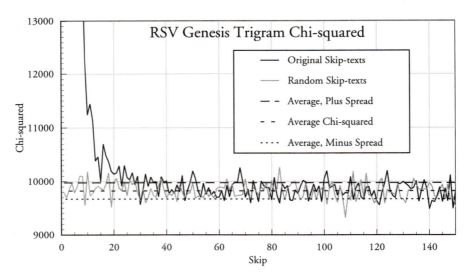

FIGURE 11.5: CHI-SQUARED ANALYSIS OF TRIGRAMS IN THE RSV TEXT OF GENESIS

look at skips greater than about 50 before the results from the original text converge with the random-text results.

Once again, we can do our averaging tricks and come up with Z-scores comparing the averages for the original text to the averages for random texts. Have a look at the results in Table 11.6. It's no big surprise that the Z-scores are all pretty small.

Notice how tiny the spreads of the entropies are. Genesis is a lot longer than *The Cat in the Hat,* and the Law of Large Numbers tells us that longer texts should have smaller spreads. That, combined with our averaging technique, gives us very high precision.

Test	Original	Random Texts	Composite Spread	Z-score
Digram Entropy	4.1356587	4.1356646	1.29E-05	-0.459
Trigram Entropy	4.1133975	4.1134172	3.60E-05	-0.547
Digram Chi-squared	535.0	533.3	4.497	0.378
Trigram Chi-squared	9835.3	9823.4	19.640	0.606

TABLE 11.6: COMBINED Z-SCORES FOR RSV TEXT OF GENESIS.

WHO CARES ABOUT ENGLISH?

You may be worried about our choice of practice texts. So far we've studied *The Cat in the Hat* and the *Revised Standard Version* of Genesis. Both of these are in English. Who cares about English? We want to study the Hebrew Bible. Won't there be some big differences in Hebrew? Hebrew hasn't got any vowels, for one thing. Won't that ruin everything?

We'll consider that question in the next chapter.

Is Hebrew Different?

So far we've studied two English texts, *The Cat in the Hat* and the *Revised Standard Version* translation of Genesis. We've shown that the skip-texts we construct from these texts are virtually indistinguishable from random texts when the skips are large (more than 50).

But how do we know that our experiments on English texts will bear any resemblance to tests done on Hebrew texts? After all, they are different languages. Hebrew doesn't have vowels. It has only 22 letters. Its letters occur with different frequencies than the corresponding letters in English.

Furthermore, isn't Hebrew supposed to be a more poetic language? Isn't it possible that it carries some sort of natural, long-range order?

These are excellent questions, and we'll work through them all in this chapter. Our first question is the very practical one of what Hebrew looks like — how its fonts and characters are represented.

The Clairmont-Michigan Representation

Much of the Internet discussion of the Bible code is in English. Because not everyone uses the same kinds of computers and not everyone has Hebrew fonts, these discussions use a common representation of the Hebrew alphabet based on standard Latin characters, the "Clairmont-Michigan" representation.

The Clairmont-Michigan representation can be a little disconcerting if you've read much real Hebrew, but it's fairly easy to get used to. It also enables non-Hebrew readers to read the texts. Since this representation seems to be the standard, we'll use it in this book.

Here is a table with the letters of the Hebrew alphabet in the Clairmont-Michigan representation. Alongside each letter we'll list the name of the letter and the nearest English equivalent. Some of the guttural Hebrew letters don't really have a good English equivalent, so consider this table an approximation.

Clairmont-Michigan Letter	Hebrew Letter Name	Equivalent English Sound
)	aleph	(none)
b	bet	b or v
g	gimel	g
d	dalet	d
h	heh	h
w	vav	v
z	zayin	z
x	het	guttural h
+	tet	t
y	yud	y
k	kaf	k or guttural k
l	lamed	l
m	mem	m
n	nun	n
s	samekh	s
(	ayin	(none)
p	peh	p or f
c	tsadi	ts
q	kuf	k
r	resh	r
$	shin	sh or s
t	tav	t

TABLE 12.1: THE CLAIRMONT-MICHIGAN REPRESENTATION OF THE HEBREW ALPHABET

Two of the letters, *aleph* and *ayin,* are listed as having no English equivalents. In fact, they aren't really pronounced at all. Technically, they're called stops. Since pronunciation of Hebrew isn't our goal, we'll say no more on this subject. The Hebrew texts we'll be analyzing are all available on my Web site in the Clairmont-Michigan representation.

TESTING WAR AND PEACE

Doron Witztum, Eliyahu Rips, and Yoav Rosenberg studied seven different texts in the Great Rabbis Experiment. One of these was the Koren edition of the Hebrew text of the book of Genesis, which has 78,064 characters. Another was the Hebrew translation of Leo Tolstoy's novel *War and Peace.* Actually, they didn't study the whole text of the novel, which is very long. Instead, they took the first 78,064 characters in order to produce a text with exactly the same number of letters as Genesis.

Witztum, Rips, and Rosenberg reported finding no Bible code in *War and Peace.* This is no great surprise. Tolstoy was a great writer, but few consider him divinely inspired. Nobody believes that the translation of his novel into Hebrew should have any special messages encoded.

We too would like to investigate this text. We expect to see something very similar to our results for the English texts.

We'll measure the digram and trigram entropies for a large number of skip-texts. We'll likewise do chi-squared analyses on our skip-texts. We expect that for large enough skips, the results will be very close to the results for random texts.

The only real question is how many skips we'll need before we reach this random behavior. For English texts, fully random behavior sets in at about 50 skips. We don't have any way to predict the exact threshold for Hebrew, but we don't have to. Our prediction is that *we'll find a threshold value.* The actual threshold itself is something we'll simply measure.

The calculations are essentially identical to those we did in chapters 10 and 11. The results are shown in Figures 12.2 through 12.5.

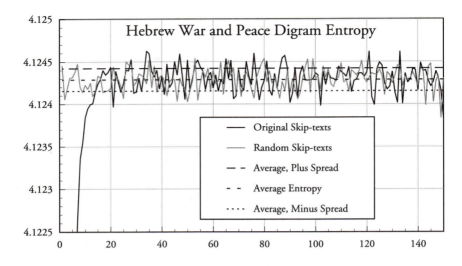

FIGURE 12.2: DIGRAM ENTROPIES OF THE HEBREW VERSION OF WAR AND PEACE

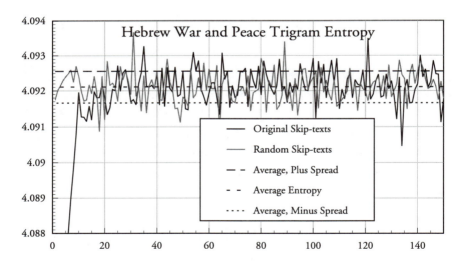

FIGURE 12.3: TRIGRAM ENTROPIES OF THE HEBREW VERSION OF WAR AND PEACE

Any surprises?

No. The plots for the original text and the plots for the random texts both jitter about, staying roughly within the horizontal lines that represent the spread. Hebrew appears to be no different in this regard from English.

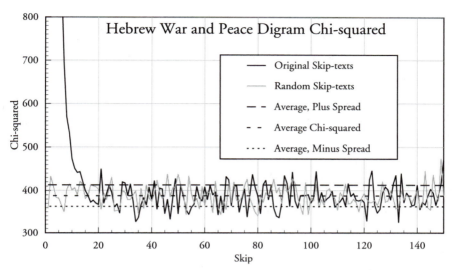

FIGURE 12.4: CHI-SQUARED ANALYSIS OF DIGRAMS IN THE HEBREW VERSION OF WAR
AND PEACE

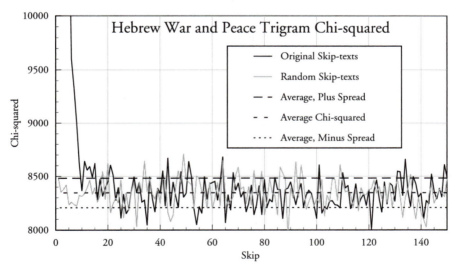

FIGURE 12.5: CHI-SQUARED ANALYSIS OF TRIGRAMS IN THE HEBREW VERSION OF WAR
AND PEACE

To be sure, the actual values of the entropy are slightly different from
English, but there is no discernible long-range order in the Hebrew text.

As in chapter 11, we'll choose a suitable threshold and average out the original skip-texts beyond that threshold. By eye, it looks like a threshold of 30 is suitable for all four tests. Also, we'll compute the average of all the random texts. Then we'll compute Z-scores to measure the difference between the two averages.

Have a look at the results in Table 12.6. In this table, we show only the Z-scores, not the actual values of entropy and chi-squared. These values have some small interest, but what we really care about is whether the skip-texts give the same values, on average, as the random texts. For that, we need only to look at the Z-scores. Please remember that each Z-score summarizes the measurements made on 300 different texts. Table 12.6 represents a lot of work!

Test	Z-score
Digram Entropy	1.276
Trigram Entropy	1.266
Digram Chi-squared	-0.9096
Trigram Chi-squared	-0.6587

TABLE 12.6: COMBINED Z-SCORES FOR HEBREW TEXT OF WAR AND PEACE

As you can see, the Z-scores are perfectly respectable. They're all less than 2. So we find no evidence for a Bible code in *War and Peace*.

Any complaints about that conclusion? I didn't think so.

So Is Hebrew Different?

Now we can answer the question we posed at the beginning of this chapter. Can we apply our tests to a Hebrew text like the Bible and get a reliable answer?

Our tests on the Hebrew text of *War and Peace* make the answer absolutely clear.

Yes! We have every reason to believe that our four tests will work just as well on the Hebrew Bible as they do on English texts.

So let's do it!

13
—

LET THERE BE LIGHT!

Genesis is a thrilling book. It has everything you're likely to find in a modern bestseller — incest and intrigue, betrayal and forgiveness, and generous doses of sex and violence. The familiar tales of the Creation and Fall and Flood lose nothing in the retelling. And the characters — the tireless Noah, the believing-yet-doubting Abraham, the cheating-and-cheated Jacob, the honest-to-a-fault Joseph — are as deep and rich as any produced by Charles Dickens.

As literature, I can think of no book quite like Genesis. It dazzles the reader as well in English as in Hebrew.

Now, as the millennium turns, a new page has been written in our understanding of Genesis. The Great Rabbis Experiment, which we discussed in chapters 3 and 4, seems to provide extraordinary new evidence that the author — no, the Author — of Genesis left His imprint as an indelible watermark within the letters of this glorious book.

In this chapter, we'll test that claim.

If you've skipped chapters 5 through 12, you've missed a lot. You won't understand what can go wrong in our experiment nor how we can protect ourselves from the errors of "postdiction." You won't know how to distinguish randomness from order using chi-squared tests. You won't know what a letter-frequency table is, nor will you know a digram from a trigram from a telegram. You won't understand entropy nor know how it can measure the redundancy in natural languages. You won't understand how long-range order in skip-texts yields evidence for intentionality. And you won't have seen how all this works out in some typical English and Hebrew texts.

In short, you'll have cheated yourself as badly as Jacob cheated Esau, and this chapter will make no more sense to you than would the speech of your co-workers on the Tower of Babel construction project.

If you've committed these sins, repent, lest you be drowned in a flood of graphs and statistics! Go back and read the chapters you've missed! Do it now, before it's too late!

LIKE THE STARS OF THE SKY

Still with us? Good. I've chased off the looky-loos. Now we can get down to business. The first thing we'll do is estimate the amount of noise in the Hebrew text of Genesis.

What do I mean by *noise?*

In communication theory, we distinguish between signal and noise. "Signal" is the message that's been communicated. "Noise" is everything else — the random garbage that we want to ignore. When you listen to the radio, the signal is the music; the noise is the background static hiss. A good radio filters out most of the noise. A bad radio may let so much noise through that you can't hear the signal.

Now, everyone agrees that the book of Genesis has noise — ELSs that are there by random chance. Christians, for example, consider the ELSs containing the name of the Reverend Sun Myung Moon to be noise. Likewise, most Jews disregard the ELSs encoding the name of Yeshua — that is, Jesus.

How can we estimate the number of meaningless ELSs that we'd expect to find in each skip-text of Genesis?

Very easily. We'll make a list of all the words that occur in the Hebrew text of Genesis. As it turns out, there are 5,003 distinct words. Most of these occur more than once in the text. The shortest words have only two letters; the longest have nine. We'll sort our list of words by length, producing a list of all the two-letter words, all the three-letter words, and so on, up to all the nine-letter words. That adds up to a total of eight lists.

Next, we'll scramble all the letters of Genesis to form a new random text. The Koren edition has 78,064 letters in it. Our scrambled text has exactly the same number. We'll look at the first two letters and check to see if they form one of our two-letter words, either forward or backward. Then we'll look at the second and third letters to see if that makes a two-letter word. We'll continue in this way through the whole scrambled text. Then we'll repeat the process, scanning for three-letter words. In this way we'll systematically search our random text for words with two, three, four…all the way up to nine letters.

My computer can do all this in just a few minutes. The results of this massive, mindless computation are shown in Table 13.1. Looking at this table, we see, for example, that Genesis has 93 distinct two-letter Hebrew words. These two-letter words occur 41,880 times in our random text. That's not terribly surprising. But notice how many words there are with four, five, or six letters!

Length of ELS	Number of Distinct Words of This Size	Number of ELSs Found in Random Text
2	93	41880
3	732	33702
4	1774	16739
5	1445	5774
6	744	1654
7	184	292
8	24	35
9	7	9
Totals	*5003*	*100085*

TABLE 13.1: SEARCH FOR MEANINGFUL WORDS IN A RANDOMIZED TEXT OF GENESIS

Why have we done this search on a *random* text? Because we wanted to find out roughly how many ELSs will occur by chance in a skip-text. We know from previous chapters that a skip-text is a lot like a random text, at least for large skips. In a random text with 78,064 letters, we've just found over 100,000 words purely by chance. Likewise, we expect that in a skip-text with 78,064 letters, we'll find about that many ELSs that form real Hebrew words. Random ELSs should run rampant!

You may wonder why we found more words than we have letters.

Remember, we scanned through the text eight different times, looking for two-letter words, three-letter words, and so on, up to nine-letter words. Also, we counted words spelled both forward and backward. So we actually scanned the text sixteen times. No wonder we found so much "noise."

In the book of Genesis, God tells Abraham to count the stars of the sky. If he could number those, then he could number his own descendants. We've found that random ELSs should be nearly as numerous, and we've barely scratched the surface. We didn't look for *all* Hebrew words; we looked only for those that happen to occur in the plain text of Genesis, a short list of only 5,003 words. Nor did we look for Hebrew spellings of Yitzhak Rabin, Indira Gandhi, or Richard Nixon. We didn't look for dates, cities, diseases, trees, chemicals, death camps, or any of the thousand other ELSs that people have found in Genesis.

Imagine what we'd find if we extended our set of words to include the vocabulary for the whole Bible, plus all of modern Hebrew, plus all Yiddish words (which are spelled with Hebrew letters), plus the names of Israeli politicians, plus transliterations of the names of all world leaders, world cities, countries, and so on. All of these words are considered fair game for searches by Bible-coders. If we made a superlist like that, with hundreds of thousands of different words, we'd find a lot of them — purely by chance — in our random text.

So, too, we'd find piles of them in skip-texts of Genesis. Purely by chance.

The lesson is clear. We have a huge amount of noise. Is there any hope of detecting a signal in all that noise?

Yes, there is, but only if there's enough signal to be "heard" above the noise.

Imagine that God has a first draft of Genesis in His mind to dictate to Moses. This draft tells the familiar stories that we all know, but it has no Bible code in it yet. Next, without altering the book's essential meaning,

He changes just enough letters to encode one new ELS waiting to be discovered in *each* skip-text.

Could we detect this single change in each skip-text?

Not really. In each skip-text, that single intentional ELS is competing for our attention with at least a hundred thousand random ELSs.

In order to get our attention, God would have to alter the text much more extensively.

My wife reminds me that God wouldn't really be sitting at the kitchen table changing letters here and there like a bad crossword-puzzler. God wouldn't even start with a first draft and make changes; He'd get it right the first time. My wife's right; she usually is. But the main point remains. If God put in a Bible code for us to find, then He would have had to encode quite a bit, or we'd never notice. He would have to devise a signal large enough to rise above all the noise.

Remember that the Bible-coders claim that God *did* encode quite a bit.

Look again at the comments by Rabbi Eliyahu ben Shlomo, which we quoted in chapter 8. Rabbi Eliyahu tells us that many details about the lives of every human, animal, and plant are encoded in the Torah. The Bible code enthusiasts interpret this to mean that a great deal of this encoded material is found as ELSs.

How much information would God need to encode in order for us to see it with the tools we've developed? Thousands of letters? Tens of thousands of letters?

That's a good question. We can estimate the answer with another simple experiment.

A SENSITIVITY TEST

The question we're asking is a common one in science. What's the smallest object your microscope can see? What's the farthest star your telescope can reach? What's the lightest particle your scale can weigh?

These are called sensitivity tests.

We want to estimate the sensitivity of our tools.

Let's restate the problem in a way that suggests the solution. Suppose we had a random text. How many letters of meaningful text could we add before our tools began detecting them?

Here's a sensitivity experiment that we can perform to answer that question. For simplicity, we'll describe an experiment for the digram entropy test. It's easy to do a similar experiment for the trigram entropy and for the chi-squared tests on digrams and trigrams.

1. We'll take the full text of Genesis and randomize it 100 times. Each time we'll measure the digram entropy. We'll average the digram entropies of all 100 random texts to estimate the expected entropy of a random text.

2. We'll repeat that first step many times, with one small change. Each time we'll *not randomize* part of the text. So we'll compute the digram entropy on a text with, say, 250 or 500 or 1,000 letters of the original text unscrambled and the remaining letters scrambled. Each of these texts we'll compare to the fully randomized results by computing a Z-score.

Why do we leave part of the text unscrambled in the second step? Because this creates a text with *some meaningful text* and a lot of purely random text. That's a lot like a skip-text with a real Bible code! (Everyone agrees that if there really were a Bible code, then any given skip-text would have lots of random ELSs and *some meaningful ELSs*.)

The experiment sketched above lets us simulate "God at the kitchen table," changing letters one by one to create more and more meaningful ELSs in thousands of skip-texts at once. In this way we can mathematically model the creation of a Bible code in any one of those skip-texts! It's not as good as fully knowing the mind of God, but who can do that? This experiment is the next best thing, at least for our limited purposes of investigating the Bible code.

In Appendix D on my Web site, there's a discussion of the exact procedure I've been using to randomize a text. Divide the text up into blocks of a certain length (typically 250 letters, but it could be almost any size). Then scramble the letters within each block. The reasons for this procedure are explained in that appendix.

In our new sensitivity experiment, we'll follow this randomization procedure, but we'll leave some blocks unscrambled. So our new text will have a few blocks with several hundred letters that form meaningful words; the remaining tens of thousands of characters will be random text.

This experiment takes several hours to run on my computer. In this calculation, as for every experiment in this book, I used a block size of 250 characters. I ran four different experiments, one each for digram entropy, trigram entropy, digram chi-squared, and trigram chi-squared. I computed the Z-scores and plotted the results in Figure 13.2.

We see clearly from this graph that as more and more characters of meaningful text are included, the digram and trigram entropies rapidly diverge from the corresponding entropies for a random text. Likewise, the chi-squared values rapidly diverge.

The trigram tests diverge faster. This means that they are more sensitive tests than the digram tests. We want to know how much meaningful text we could add before our tests clearly diverge from random chance. Let's be very conservative in our estimates. We'll insist that the Z-score has

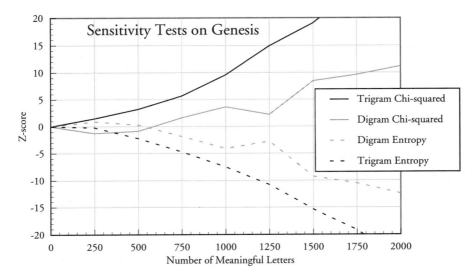

FIGURE 13.2: FOUR SENSITIVITY TESTS ON PARTIALLY RANDOMIZED TEXTS OF GENESIS

to exceed 5. As you know, a Z-score of 5 is huge. It would happen by chance barely 3 times in 10 million.

As you can see from the plots, the digram tests reach a Z-score of 5 when about 1,400 letters of meaningful text have been added, that is, only about 2 percent of the total text! The trigram tests reach that same Z-score after adding 700 letters, only 1 percent of the total text.

This is remarkable. Imagine God sitting at His kitchen table changing letters. After He's changed only 1 percent of the text, He has left an enormous signature for us to find in our trigram tests. After He's changed only 2 percent of the text, He's stamped a fingerprint a mile wide on all four of our tests! We can't miss it.

If many ELSs are encoded, we can't miss them.

Of course, God doesn't have a kitchen table, and He didn't change letters one by one. If He wrote the Bible code, He undoubtedly wrote it in one step, not hundreds or thousands. *But the effect is the same.* It doesn't matter whether He added the Bible code bit by bit or created it all at once. The result would be all those encoded skip-texts, each with thousands of meaningful ELSs, leaving God's signature in the Bible as clearly as if He'd written it in fiery letters in the night sky.

If the signature is there, our tests are powerful enough to find it.

In our experiments so far on *The Cat in the Hat,* the RSV text of Genesis, and the Hebrew translation of *War and Peace,* we've seen essentially no signal at all, as reflected in the graphs in chapters 10 through 12. For large enough skips, the entropies and chi-squared values of both digrams and trigram probabilities converge to the corresponding values for random texts.

If there is a Bible code in the Bible, what do we expect to find? Figure 13.3 shows a plot of digram entropies for a hypothetical text with a Bible code in it. (To create this plot, I modified the real data from *War and Peace* by hand.) Even for large values of the skip, the entropy of this "coded" text is clearly different from the entropy of a random text.

If we see a plot like this in our tests on Genesis, then we'll have powerful evidence for a Bible code.

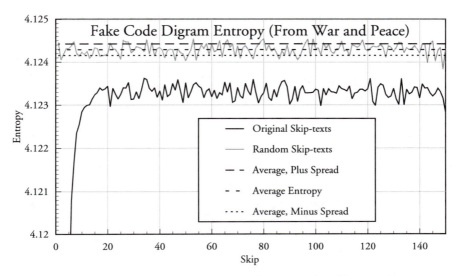

FIGURE 13.3: WHAT WE'D SEE IF THERE WERE A "BIBLE CODE" IN WAR AND PEACE

There. I've made a prediction. The prediction is based on our past observations and simple logic. Now it's time to test that prediction.

The stage is set. The cameras are ready. The actors are suffering terminal stage fright.

Let's roll!

TESTING THE BIBLE CODE IN GENESIS

Picture the setting as I prepared to run the tests on Genesis. I'd written my software, had run it on the texts we've studied so far in this book, and had made final preparations to run it on Genesis.

Then I staged a party. I invited a number of fellow writers, members of my Hebrew class, and friends who'd suffered through my endless talk about the Bible code for months. Several of them were technical folk — physicists, engineers, programmers. Most weren't. My eight-year-old daughter Gracie was an active participant.

I set up my computer in the living room, packed everyone in, and gave a lecture on the Bible code. You've already seen the contents of that lecture in the first twelve chapters of this book. At the end of the lecture, I made a prediction.

If there is a Bible code in Genesis, I said, then we ought to see a graph that looks like the one shown in Figure 13.3. If there's no Bible code, then we'll see graphs like those in chapters 10 through 12.

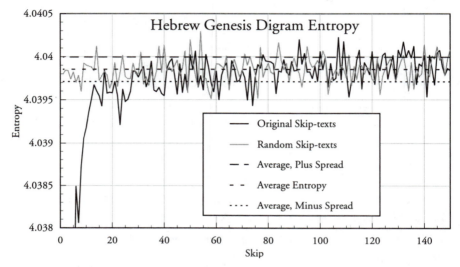

FIGURE 13.4: DIGRAM ENTROPIES OF THE KOREN TEXT OF GENESIS

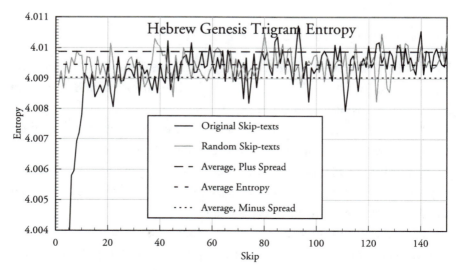

FIGURE 13.5: TRIGRAM ENTROPIES OF THE KOREN TEXT OF GENESIS

I fired up the digram entropy program, entered the information needed to run the software, and pressed the button to start the analysis. Two minutes and twenty-nine seconds later, the program finished executing.

I've plotted the results of that first run in Figure 13.4.

Is there a Bible code in the Koren text of Genesis? You be the judge. If

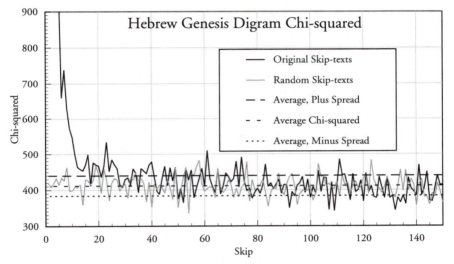

FIGURE 13.6: CHI-SQUARED ANALYSIS OF DIGRAMS IN THE KOREN TEXT OF GENESIS

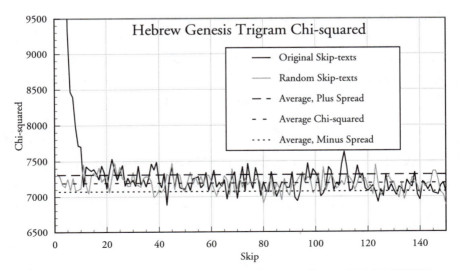

FIGURE 13.7: CHI-SQUARED ANALYSIS OF TRIGRAMS IN THE KOREN TEXT OF GENESIS

I've done my job correctly, you have all the information you need to make your own decision.

Let's do the other tests too. I've plotted the results of our other three tests in Figures 13.5 through 13.7.

Just as we did in chapters 11 and 12, we can combine the results of all the random texts and all the skip-texts from the original (past a threshold skip of 50) into a single Z-score. The results, which summarize Figures 13.4 through 13.7, are shown below in Table 13.8.

Test	Z-score
Digram Entropy	0.300
Digram Chi-squared	-0.205
Trigram Entropy	1.110
Trigram Chi-squared	-0.751

TABLE 13.8: COMBINED Z-SCORES FOR HEBREW TEXT OF GENESIS

I think the results are unambiguous. Do you agree?

THE TRUTH ABOUT THE BIBLE CODE

The results of the computation on Genesis convinced everyone at the party, believers and skeptics alike. Some were sorry; some were glad. I'd have been happy either way. But my personal feelings don't really matter. To put it bluntly, neither do yours. What matters is the truth. The truth is that there isn't any scientific evidence for the Bible code in Genesis. Zip. Zero. Zilch.

But there's more to the story than Genesis. People have claimed to find remarkable ELSs in other books of the Bible. We still need to analyze the rest of the Torah and then the whole Hebrew Bible.

We turn to that analysis next. Don't fall asleep. There's a little surprise waiting for the unwary.

14

THE REST OF THE STORY

We're not done yet. True, we've found powerful evidence that the results of the Great Rabbis Experiment were invalid and that Genesis has no intentional messages encoded as ELSs.

Still, there is more to examine. We'd like to look at the rest of the Hebrew Bible, especially the rest of the Torah. And we have a couple of loose threads just begging to be yanked on.

Let's take care of those first since they're easy.

CONCOCTING OUR OWN BIBLE CODE

One of my friends at the party, physicist Jay R. Hill, suggested the following experiment. Build a fake Bible-code text that contains the full text of *The Cat in the Hat* at some skip-count. Then run my software on this text and see what happens.

I took an evening, wrote a Bible-code-maker program, and ran *The Cat in the Hat* through it to create what looked like a random mess. Here are the first few lines of it, for your amusement:

```
tlnoeeoattoodahoaealeldch
neobmsamoiethnftyyatkowhn
aawoenrenehahtnopywumbrku
khndmeasdenihoswdeaatedhw
htdlcbktiimwiyaurhlpcloaa
dlwoaituudinietaioswtxieg
```

This may look random, but it's not. The full text of *The Cat in the Hat* is embedded in this at a skip-count of 100. We expect that at any skip other than 100, our analysis should look just like random text. But at a skip of 100, it will look wildly different. Let's test that right now. We'll make the usual digram entropy calculation, 150 skip-texts and 150 random texts for comparison. In Figure 14.1, I've plotted the results.

As you can see, the random texts and the skip-texts from the modified version agree with each other within the spread, except at one skip-count. The plot has a huge "spike" at a skip of 100. That's exactly what we expected.

No surprises here. The software works perfectly. What's next?

A LAST LONG LOOK AT GENESIS

Another suggestion made at the party was to run my software for a really long time. Most of my computations have gone out to 150 skips. But why stop there? Why not take it out to 2,000 skips?

There's no good reason, other than that it takes quite a bit longer. I

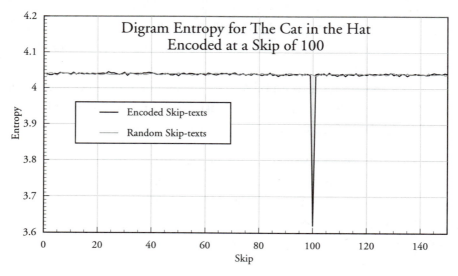

FIGURE 14.1: DIGRAM ENTROPY OF FAKED BIBLE CODE CONTAINING THE CAT IN THE HAT

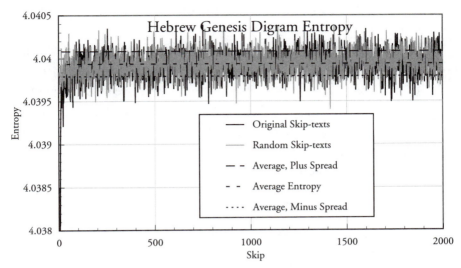

FIGURE 14.2: DIGRAM ENTROPY OF THE HEBREW TEXT OF GENESIS FOR 2,000 SKIPS

didn't expect to see much new, but I figured it would be a good exercise for the software.

Figure 14.2 shows the results of the digram entropy calculation.

This plot is pretty crowded, but it shows absolutely no deviation from random behavior. As usual, we can compare the average of the random texts to the average of those original skip-texts with skips greater than 50. The Z-score is -1.334. This is perfectly normal. So for skip-texts up to about 2,000, there is no evidence of a Bible code. We could go to higher skips, but I don't see any real reason to do so.

Of course, that still leaves the rest of the Torah. Isn't it possible that Exodus, Leviticus, Numbers, or Deuteronomy might have a Bible code even if Genesis doesn't? Yes, it's possible. In fact, I can guarantee we'll see something interesting in at least one of the books.

WEIRD NUMBERS

Some of you are probably smirking right now, because you see what's coming. If you've read the book of Numbers recently (and who hasn't?), you'll recall that there's an extremely repetitive section in chapter 7, verses 12 through 83.

This passage follows the same six-verse pattern twelve times in a row, once for each tribe of Israel. In each six-verse block, the first verse mentions a leader from one of the twelve tribes. Then the next five describe an offering of a silver plate, a silver sprinkling bowl, and so on. These five verses, by my count, contain 206 letters total. They are repeated, word for word, for each of the twelve tribes. Read it and enjoy.

I remember reading this section in Hebrew some time ago and thinking that it was going to set off one massive signal in my software. Here's why.

We have a chunk of 206 letters, repeated 12 times. Now consider the skip-text of Numbers at a skip of, say, 100. Letters 1 and 101 in that big chunk are going to form a digram that we can guarantee will occur at least 12 times in the text. Likewise, letters 2 and 102 will make a digram that will also occur at least 12 times. This continues all the way up to the digram formed by letters 106 and 206.

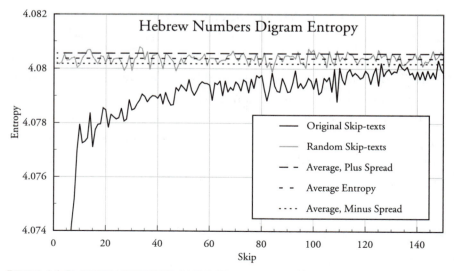

FIGURE 14.3: DIGRAM ENTROPIES IN THE KOREN TEXT OF NUMBERS

So in this skip-text, we have 106 different digrams that will occur at least 12 times. Now some of these may be common digrams, but some will be rare. With 106 different possibilities, there's a high likelihood that several of them will be quite rare. But they won't be rare in our skip-text! They'll each occur at least 12 times.

So we're almost guaranteed to skew the digram tables, and that's bound to show up in our digram entropy test and our digram chi-squared test. Likewise, the trigram tests will show abnormal, nonrandom behavior.

The same thing will happen at all skip-texts less than about 200!

So we're guaranteed to see a "signal" similar to a real Bible code. Let's have a look at the digram entropy analysis of Numbers in Figure 14.3.

Clearly, the skip-text digram entropy for the original is well below the random digram entropy. Statistically, the deviation is highly significant.

But it doesn't mean anything.

How can I say that so confidently? How can I be sure that all of the signal is due to that one passage in chapter 7 of Numbers?

It's easy to prove. We'll snip out that section, Numbers 7:12-83, and run it through a scrambler. The scrambled text will have exactly the same letters as the original, but it no longer has blocks of 206 characters repeated 12 times. Now we'll put the scrambled text back into the original.

The result is something we'll call MixedNumbers. It's identical to the original text, except in the long section we've been complaining about, which is now thoroughly random.

Next we run our usual analysis on MixedNumbers. The results for the digram entropies are shown in Figure 14.4.

The "signal" has completely disappeared! We conclude that it was spurious, caused by the repetitive section in Numbers 7.

A final check is to run the analysis on the original text of Numbers out beyond skips of 206. We expect that the entropy will approach random behavior soon thereafter. The results of this calculation are plotted in Figure 14.5.

Just as expected, the digram entropy becomes random for skips higher than about 200.

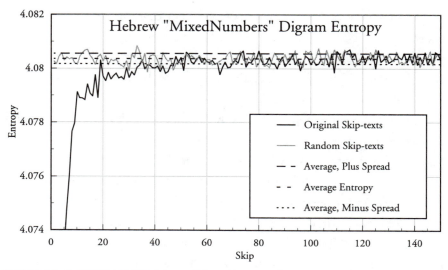

FIGURE 14.4: DIGRAM ENTROPIES IN "MIXEDNUMBERS"

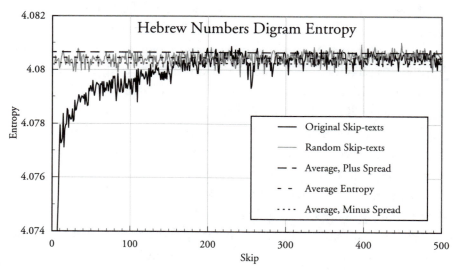

FIGURE 14.5: DIGRAM ENTROPIES IN NUMBERS OUT TO 500 SKIPS

There is no evidence of a Bible code in Numbers. Our software is very sensitive. It detected a block of 206 letters repeated 12 times. Is there any doubt that it could have found a Bible code if there were one?

Let's keep looking. Something may turn up.

THE REST OF THE TORAH

In this section, we're going to examine the rest of the Torah.

By now, you've probably seen enough plots to last you a lifetime. There's no real reason to show so much information anymore. If you've seen a few dozen of these plots, you've pretty much seen them all. So from now on, I'm just going to summarize the results.

What we really want to know is whether the results for skip-texts from the original text deviate from random behavior. As we discussed in chapter 11, we can summarize the results of any of our four tests very simply. First, we combine the results of all the random texts to get an average value and a spread. Second, we choose some threshold skip, say 50, and combine the results of all original skip-texts beyond that point to get an average and a spread. Do the two averages agree within the deviation expected by the two spreads? To decide that, we just have to compute a Z-score, as we explained in chapter 11.

If the Z-score is "small," then we have to conclude that the two averages agree. As we saw in chapters 11 and 12, "small" means less than about 3.

Table 14.6 summarizes the results of 24 different calculations I've made on the Torah (including the "patched-up" text of Numbers that we've been calling MixedNumbers).

The Z-scores are small for all the texts except Numbers, and we already understand why Numbers gives large results. MixedNumbers does not.

Text	Digram Entropy	Trigram Entropy	Digram Chi-squared	Trigram Chi-squared
Genesis	0.300	1.110	-0.205	-0.751
Exodus	-1.636	-0.072	1.579	1.733
Leviticus	-0.909	0.032	1.373	0.167
Numbers	-32.722	-32.084	36.496	44.614
MixedNumbers	-1.915	0.491	2.160	0.228
Deuteronomy	-0.220	0.973	0.341	-1.341

TABLE 14.6: SUMMARY OF Z-SCORES FOR ALL ANALYSES ON THE TORAH

There seems to be no room for doubt. The ELSs found in the Torah are precisely those we would expect due to random chance.

There is no Bible code in the Torah.

Of course, people have claimed to find codes in other books of the Hebrew Bible. Very well, let's keep going.

THE REST OF THE HEBREW BIBLE

We've already seen that the Torah has no Bible code. I've run the digram entropy test on the rest of the Hebrew Bible to see if anything pops up. As before, we'll be interested in the Z-score. The results are shown in Table 14.7.

The results are very clear. Not one of the Z-scores is even as high as 3, although the tiny book of Obadiah just misses it, and the Song of Songs is also a bit higher than normal. But none of the books is wildly far from random — enough to warrant a further search.

WHAT HAVE WE PROVED?

Let's now summarize what we've proved in the last two chapters. It's important to keep in mind how our methods are different from those used by both the proponents and the critics of the Bible code.

The believers have typically taken the following approach (with the possible exception of the Great Rabbis Experiment):

1. Look for an "amazing pattern" in the Bible.

2. Calculate the probability that such a pattern could have occurred by chance.

3. Conclude that God (or space aliens) encoded the pattern for us to find.

The skeptics have generally attacked this line of argument by noting (correctly) that this is postdiction. We discussed what's wrong with postdiction in chapter 5.

However, I can't help thinking that many critics of the Bible code are guilty of something similar. Much of their criticism begins from one of the following three (unprovable) assumptions:

Test	Z-score
Joshua	-0.260
Judges	0.928
Ruth	-0.231
1 Samuel	-1.409
2 Samuel	0.937
1 Kings	-0.560
2 Kings	1.119
1 Chronicles	-1.529
2 Chronicles	0.173
Ezra	0.883
Nehemiah	-0.243
Esther	0.023
Job	-0.049
Psalms	-0.091
Proverbs	0.846
Ecclesiastes	-0.715
Song of Songs	-2.588
Isaiah	-1.713
Jeremiah	-0.871
Lamentations	-1.577
Ezekiel	-0.835
Daniel	-0.002
Hosea	-1.661
Joel	-0.646
Amos	-0.648
Obadiah	-2.961
Jonah	-0.487
Micah	-1.023
Nahum	1.862
Habakkuk	1.913
Zephaniah	-1.929
Haggai	-0.551
Zechariah	0.249
Malachi	-0.128

TABLE 14.7: SUMMARY OF DIGRAM ENTROPY ANALYSES ON OTHER BOOKS IN THE HEBREW BIBLE

1. God does not exist.

2. God exists, but He wouldn't hide secret information in the Torah.

3. The Torah we now have is so different from the original that a Bible code could not have survived to the present day.

The problem with these assumptions is that not everybody accepts them. Therefore, the believers and skeptics lack common ground for discussion, so the debate degenerates into *ad hominem* arguments or worse.

In this book, I've made none of these assumptions. Instead, I've based everything on two fundamental assertions:

1. If information is encoded, then it must differ from random text. (Otherwise, how could we detect it?)

2. If information is encoded as ELSs, then it must be encoded at many different skips. (Otherwise, not much information could be encoded.)

The believers typically search for some small subset of the nearly infinite set of all possible words. That's too fuzzy. In this book we've recognized that all words are made up of simple building blocks — digrams and trigrams. There is a finite number of distinct digrams and trigrams, and we can therefore study them *completely and rapidly*. We have systematically searched hundreds of skip-texts in each of many different texts, scanning for any deviation from randomness.

We have found nonrandom behavior in only two places:

1. For small skips in all the texts we analyzed, the digrams and trigrams are not random. Statistically, this is very significant for skips less than about 10. For skips between 10 and 50 it is just noticeable. For skips greater than about 50, the original skip-texts are indistinguishable from random text.

2. The book of Numbers is the only exception. It shows nonrandom behavior for skips out to about 200, the length of the longest block of repeating text. Beyond that, skip-texts from Numbers look fully random.

Our sensitivity tests tell us that if any group of skip-texts held more than a 1-percent encoded message, we would detect an *enormous* signal. However, *we detect no significant signal at all.*

If there really is a Bible code, then it must be in one of two places:

1. At skips less than 10, where my tests can't measure randomness

because of the short-range order of the language. (But compare the graphs of the Bible to the graphs for the other texts we've studied. Qualitatively, they look similar even at small skips. Even though I don't know how to analyze the small skip-texts statistically, my eyes see no pattern at all.)

2. At skips greater than 10, there might be a very tiny number of ELSs encoded. (But it would be impossible ever to decide which are the real thing among the vast sea of random ELSs.)

The verdict is in.

WHO WROTE THE BIBLE CODE?

Since chapter 1, I've been promising to answer the question that forms the title of this book: *Who wrote the Bible code?*

By now, you already know my answer. Nobody wrote the Bible code. There is no Bible code.

One question remains. If there is no Bible code, then how do we explain all the strange findings reported by others?

We turn to that question in the next three chapters.

15

THE SIGNATURE OF YESHUA?

As the daddy of three girls, I get invited to a lot of birthday parties. Usually I'm not exactly a guest; I'm the chauffeur for my daughters.

So you can understand how delighted I was when Joy, one of my young friends, asked me a week before her fourth birthday, "Randy! Are you coming to my birthday party?"

I wondered just how clear she was on the concept of a birthday party. "Sure, Joy," I said. "I'd like to come if I can. Do you know how old you're going to be?"

"Of course!" Joy puffed out her chest with pride. "I'm going to be *four and a half!*"

That was several years ago. Joy doesn't remember this episode now. I can't forget it.

Children often make naive statements because they don't know any better. We forgive them because they're cute.

Adults make naive statements for the same reason. They don't know any better. All too often, we don't forgive them, because adults generally aren't cute and we think they ought to know better.

The fact is, nobody can "know better" about every mistake they make. If you spend your life trying to avoid saying anything naive, you may end up never saying a thing. And the rest of us might miss out on the insights that only you have. That'd be a shame.

I say all this as preface to my investigation of the work of Yacov Rambsel. Rambsel has rocked a few boats in the last couple of years, claiming to find "Yeshua" encoded as ELSs in messianic passages of the Hebrew

Bible. Rambsel believes that these ELSs prove that Jesus of Nazareth is the Messiah. I want to discuss his claims in this chapter since a number of persons have criticized him as being naive in the extreme.

First, we need to discuss a rather touchy subject. I'll be brief.

JEWS, JESUS, AND JUDAISM

Yacov Rambsel is a Messianic rabbi; that is, he's the spiritual leader of a congregation of Jews who believe Jesus is the Messiah. Now I'm all too aware that mainstream Judaism utterly rejects Messianic Judaism, and I understand the reasons why. Relations between Jews and Christians have been very rocky for nearly two millennia, and Christians have been the aggressors far more often than not. Countless Jews have been murdered in the name of Jesus, under the sign of the cross. Others have been forcibly converted to Christianity. Some have been forced to convert and *then* have been murdered.

Because of this long and ugly history, Rambsel's alleged "Yeshua codes" have jabbed at an open wound in the Jewish consciousness. But it's not only his work that offends. It's also his self-identification as a Messianic Jew, which most Jews see as a contradiction in terms.

Jewish authors have answered Rambsel's claims at length in articles posted on the Internet. In these articles, they consistently call him "Pastor Rambsel," which is their way of saying that he's not really Jewish, he's a Christian. These articles bristle with an undercurrent of anger.

That's unfortunate, because some Christians read these articles, see the emotional undercurrent, and discount the logic. To these readers, the authors' anti-Messianic bias taints the message.

I don't think anyone can call me biased against Messianic Jews. I've studied Hebrew and have enjoyed the music and liturgy at a Messianic Jewish congregation here in San Diego for several years. I'm not a member, but I find it a terrific place to learn more about Judaism and to study Hebrew. I like Messianic Jews, although I don't agree with every single one of their beliefs.

That said, I have some very bad news for Yacov Rambsel. His critics are right. His findings have no statistical value at all.

YACOV RAMBSEL'S EVIDENCE

Yacov Rambsel's first book, *Yeshua*, was published in the fall of 1996. The main point of his book was that the Hebrew name "Yeshua" is found encoded in many passages of the Hebrew Bible that Christians consider messianic prophecies.

I've worded that last sentence carefully. Mainstream Jews don't agree that most of these passages refer to the Messiah. Predictably, the Jewish response to Rambsel was swift. Rabbi Daniel Mechanic, a senior lecturer for the Discovery Seminar sponsored by the Jewish organization Aish HaTorah (Flame of Torah), attacked Rambsel's findings in an article entitled "Jesus Codes: Uses and Abuses," posted on several Web sites.

Rabbi Mechanic begins by pointing out that every text has words that appear as ELSs — millions of them. If you've read chapter 13 of this book, then you know that Mechanic is correct. We randomized the text of Genesis and found more than 100,000 words embedded in that text, counting overlaps and reversed words. We could have found many more by enlarging the set of words to search for. For an original text of this size, any skip-text should have hundreds of thousands of ELSs just by random chance, and there would be thousands of skip-texts to check!

Very often, Rabbi Mechanic says, ELSs in the Bible are random. They should be considered mere coincidences until proven otherwise. However, he believes that the Great Rabbis Experiment provides evidence that some ELSs in Genesis are not random but represent genuine "Bible codes."

Mechanic then points out that the four Hebrew letters that spell "Yeshua," namely *yud-shin-vav-ayin*, are common letters. He shows that "Yeshua" appears as an ELS thousands of times in both the Torah and the Hebrew translation of *War and Peace*. Indeed, so do "Mohammed," "Krishna," "Koresh," and "Moon." Are all of these messiahs? Of course not.

Mechanic then challenges Rambsel (along with Grant Jeffrey, Yacov

Rambsel's friend and original publisher) to submit their findings to an unbiased panel of experts.

Now there really isn't any such thing as an unbiased expert, although there *are* plenty of experts. Some believe in God. Some don't. Some haven't decided. Each of these positions is a bias. We're all biased. The best we can do is to use scientific method to try to remove the effects of our biases.

I've seen no scientific evidence for the validity of Rambsel's claims. Not only that, we've found hard scientific evidence in chapters 13 and 14 of this book that *no such evidence is possible.* We measured the frequencies of digrams and trigrams — the building blocks of all meaningful words. Those frequencies in the biblical texts are precisely what we expect to see by random chance alone. The Yeshua codes are no more meaningful than my discovery of "Amy" in the alphabet in chapter 2.

BEYOND THE YESHUA CODES

In 1997 Rambsel published a second book, *His Name Is Jesus,* with more "evidence" for the Yeshua codes. This book expands the search from "Yeshua" to a long list of other names and words related to Jesus.

On page 62 of the original edition of that book, Rambsel seems surprised that anyone would doubt the significance of his findings. Yet he presents no scientific evidence at all.

Instead, he issues a challenge to his critics. On pages 63 and 64, he presents a list of words that are encoded at "small" skips in the Suffering Servant passage in Isaiah 53. The great majority of the ELSs on his list are at skips between 10 and 300.

On Rambsel's list we find such words as "Yeshua," "Nazarene," "Messiah," and so on. Most of the twelve disciples are included. For some reason, "Judas" isn't on the list. But "Seed" is. So is "Water." Also some long phrases, like "From the Atonement Lamb" and "Let Him be crucified."

Rambsel challenges his critics to find all of these words and phrases in any other Hebrew passage of the same length as the Isaiah passage. If no one can do this, he believes, then that will provide powerful evidence that he is right, "that these codes are truly unprecedented."

That claim is charmingly naive.

Suppose you decide to take a section of the Tel Aviv phone book and start looking for Rambsel's list of words. You find "Yeshua" easily enough, since it's a common ELS. In fact, you find it several times. You find "Nazarene" and "Messiah," too.

And so you march down the list, checking off the words. To your surprise, you also find "Judas." Interesting. You begin to feel a little irritated with Rambsel. He apparently failed to find "Judas," but you're not allowed to criticize his failure, because he's the one defining success. Success means that you have to find exactly the words on his list.

You continue on until you reach Rambsel's phrase "the evil Roman city." You can't find this ELS!

Failure! You lose Rambsel's challenge.

Now you're feeling upset. It's not fair! This is a long phrase, and it's not reasonable to expect to find it in such a short passage. Then you spot something in your own text that sets your blood pumping. There's a hot one! "Crucified Son of God."

But then you realize that you just got lucky. You found a random phrase in the Tel Aviv phone book. It's not a Bible code and you know it. You reach for your Hebrew copy of Genesis and start looking. You don't find either of the above long phrases, but now you find a new one. "Yeshua, crucified Lion of God." Wow! Isn't that great? That must be a Bible code.

Well, no, not by the test Rambsel proposed for you. Now you're angry. You've found a terrific Bible code, but it's not on Rambsel's list, so it doesn't count! And you didn't find the ones that were on his list, so you flunk! His challenge ends up "invalidating" Genesis!

With an effort you calm down and decide to issue a counterchallenge. You ask Yacov Rambsel to find *your* pet phrases in the book of Isaiah. After all, if you have to pass his test, then he ought to have to pass yours.

I guarantee that he can't. Here's why. If we all go looking in different texts, we'll find words and phrases by chance. Lots of words. Several phrases. In each text we'll find a different set.

There'll be some overlap, of course. Most of us will find short words like "Yeshua" or "Mary" in our texts. Maybe I'll find "Lamb of God." Maybe you'll find "Let Him be crucified." Maybe our sacrilegious neighbor will find "John Lennon, Alligator of God."

Do any of these findings mean anything?

As we said in chapter 2, maybe so, maybe not. The only way to tell is to gather statistical information and compare it to the expected results based on random chance. If I expect to see "Yeshua" a thousand times in my text, and I find it ten thousand times, that's a surprise. That's huge, in fact.

But that's not the sort of evidence Yacov Rambsel is giving us.

It's tempting to get angry at him, but let's just stick to the dull, boring facts. The simple fact is that neither of Yacov Rambsel's books contains any statistical information that would be useful to a scientist. (Yes, I've read chapters 8 and 11 of his book *Yeshua,* in which he tries to calculate probabilities. His calculations have too much wiggle room to have any hard scientific value.)

Now it may be that Rambsel's findings, which he calls "insights," are meaningful to him as a believer. They edify him and possibly others. I have no complaint with that.

But please don't call it evidence. And please don't call it a "Yeshua code." A code implies that it is meaningful, not random. I have seen no evidence of a Yeshua code in Isaiah or any other book of the Hebrew Bible. No evidence, period.

COINCIDENCE

You may still be wondering how we explain Rambsel's findings. After all, some of the phrases he's found are rare. Some of them have very low probabilities of occurring in a text the size of Isaiah 53. So why do we find them?

We discussed the basic ideas back in chapter 5.

There are a lot of interesting phrases we could search for, similar to the ones Rambsel found. By varying the words and scrambling the word order, we could think of many thousands of interesting phrases relating to Jesus. Most of them are extremely improbable. Let's say, to keep the math simple, that each phrase would be expected to happen only once in a thousand times in a passage of a given size.

Now suppose we make a list of ten thousand phrases to search for. We'd expect to find about ten of them. But we'd also find about ten of them in an equal-sized section of *War and Peace,* the Tel Aviv phone book, or *The Celestine Prophecy.*

Most likely we'd be finding a different set each time. But we'd almost certainly find a few *if we looked for enough different phrases.*

That's the secret. Just look long enough, don't report your failures, and you can always get "amazing results."

It's called coincidence.

The only way to prove that a coincidence means something is to do the dull statistical work that I've forced my computer to do for us in this book.

The Yeshua codes don't mean anything. They are coincidences, nothing more. If coincidences edify you, then read Yacov Rambsel's books and enjoy. Just don't be surprised if those coincidences don't edify your neighbor.

But What About...?

But what about the Great Rabbis Experiment? In that case, Doron Witztum, Eliyahu Rips, and Yoav Rosenberg have done some very complex statistical analysis, and they claim amazing results. They quote a very low probability that their findings could be coincidence. Are they mistaken? If so, then where did they go wrong?

That question will require a whole chapter of its own. As my friend Joy would say, please turn to chapter 16 and a half.

16

How Do We Explain the Great Rabbis Experiment?

We discussed the Great Rabbis Experiment early in this book and promised to do some mathematical analysis of it later. In chapter 6 we developed an excellent tool for the job — the chi-squared analysis. We've seen the value of chi-squared throughout this book. Now let's apply it to the Great Rabbis Experiment.

CHI-SQUARED ANALYSIS OF THE GREAT RABBIS EXPERIMENT

The following analysis is based on the original paper by Doron Witztum, Eliyahu Rips, and Yoav Rosenberg, which appeared in the August 1994 issue of *Statistical Science*. (See the exact reference in the bibliography.) You can find the article posted on various Bible-code Web sites, and it's also included as an appendix in Michael Drosnin's book *The Bible Code*. Be forewarned that it uses rather formidable-looking mathematical formulae. I can vouch, however, that the math makes sense.

Let's spell out exactly what Witztum, Rips, and Rosenberg did, and then we'll show why their results are so surprising.

1. They defined a "distance function." The function provides a measure of the distance between any two ELSs in a text.

2. They defined a statistical measure of the average distance between the "most significant" ELS occurrences of a given pair of words.

3. They identified a number of "word-pairs." In each pair, one word was the name or abbreviation for a famous rabbi. The other "word" was the Hebrew encoding of the birth date or death date of that rabbi.

4. They applied the statistical measure of average closeness to their word-pairs and checked to see if the results were random.

They performed this experiment twice. The first time, they used those rabbis whose biographical entries contained at least three columns of text in Margalioth's *Encyclopedia of Great Men in Israel.* The second time, they used those rabbis who merited more than one and a half columns of text but fewer than three. As a check of their results, they ran the experiment on both the actual text of Genesis, labeled in their paper "G," and a random text, labeled "R."

For each of the tests, Witztum, Rips, and Rosenberg found somewhere between 152 and 165 word-pairs that could be tested for closeness. They adjusted their "closeness" measure to be a number between 0 and 1. Then they made a histogram (a bar graph showing frequency distribution) with bins of width 0.04. This gave them 25 bins. You'd expect slightly more than 6 word-pairs to be found in each bin, with a spread of about 2.5. This

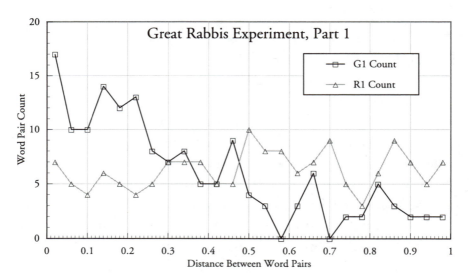

FIGURE 16.1: NUMBER OF WORD-PAIRS AT VARIOUS DISTANCES IN TEXTS R1 AND G1

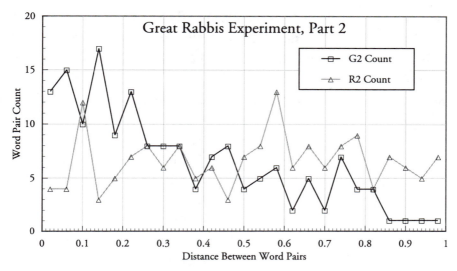

FIGURE 16.2: NUMBER OF WORD-PAIRS AT VARIOUS DISTANCES IN TEXTS R2 AND G2

means that some bins might reasonably have no entries, and some might have as many as 13 or so.

Let's study the results of these experiments, taken from Figure 4 of the *Statistical Science* paper. I've plotted their numbers in Figures 16.1 and 16.2. The horizontal axis represents their statistical measure of average closeness. The vertical axis is the number of word-pairs at each distance.

If the word-pairs were randomly distributed, then the plots should be approximately flat. That is, some word-pairs would be "close together" and some would be "far apart."

That's exactly what we see for the curves labeled R1 and R2, the results of the two tests on the random text. It's not, however, what we see for the curves labeled G1 and G2, the corresponding results for Genesis. For tests G1 and G2, the word-pairs are far more often "close" to each other than far away.

A chi-squared analysis makes all this mathematically precise. Table 16.3 summarizes the results of chi-squared analyses of tests G1, G2, R1, and R2. The probabilities shown give the likelihood that the chi-squared value could be so large by random chance. See on my Web site Appendix B, equations

(B6) and (B7), for the mathematics behind these probability estimates. If this probability is greater than 0.01, it's generally considered reasonable to dismiss the results as random. We'll regard probabilities to be interesting if they're less than 0.01 and very significant if they fall below 0.001. The smaller the probabilities, the greater the significance.

Text	Chi-squared	Probability	Significant?
G1	86.664	5.1E-09	Yes
G2	77.684	1.4E-07	Yes
R1	11.783	0.982	No
R2	22.412	0.555	No

TABLE 16.3: RESULTS OF CHI-SQUARED ANALYSES ON THE GREAT RABBIS EXPERIMENT

Both the tests R1 and R2 give completely normal values of chi-squared for text R, the random text. We conclude, in agreement with Witztum, Rips, and Rosenberg, that the random text R has no Bible code.

But the chi-squared values for tests G1 and G2 on Genesis are very large! Both probabilities are much less than one in a million. That is stunning.

The odds of both the G1 and G2 plots having such large chi-squared values are extremely small. Once again we are forced to agree with Witztum, Rips, and Rosenberg that this did not happen by chance.

But did God do it? (Or little green men?) I think not.

WHO'S RIGHT?

We now have two sets of results that don't agree. The Great Rabbis Experiment finds a result that is very unlikely to have happened by random chance. Our experiments in chapters 13 and 14 indicate that the skip-texts of Genesis are completely random (for large enough skips).

We can't both be right.

As discussed in chapter 4, Professor Barry Simon has written articles on the Bible code, which you can read on his Web site. In "The Case Against the Codes," he talks about the "wiggle room" in the Great Rabbis Experiment.

By "wiggle room," Professor Simon means that Witztum, Rips, and Rosenberg had some freedom in choosing the spellings used for the names of rabbis. This would allow them to choose those spellings that gave good results. This idea is illustrated by an article written by Professors Dror Bar-Natan and Brendan McKay. In their paper, "Equidistant Letter Sequences in Tolstoy's 'War and Peace,'" posted on McKay's Web site, they chose a slightly different set of rabbis and different spellings for some of the names used in the Great Rabbis Experiment.

The result?

Bar-Natan and McKay found a "Bible code" in the text of *War and Peace* but none in Genesis! Of course, they manipulated the spellings to get the result they wanted. That was their point. They concluded that Witztum, Rips, and Rosenberg *could have likewise manipulated their own experiment.*

In chapter 4, I argued that this, by itself, is not good enough. "Could have" is not the same as "did." Where is the empirical evidence against the Great Rabbis Experiment?

At last, we have an answer. The empirical evidence is right here in this book. We've seen powerful evidence that the Great Rabbis Experiment should have yielded null results. In fact, our evidence shows that *any experiment like the Great Rabbis Experiment should fail.* I conclude that somehow, some way, wiggle room has corrupted the Great Rabbis Experiment.

Please note that this does not mean Witztum, Rips, and Rosenberg are dishonest. No, I don't believe that. All the evidence tells me that they believe very deeply in their results and that they've made an honest effort to get the right answer. Yet I still think their experiments are incorrect.

WHERE COULD THEY HAVE GONE WRONG?

You may be wondering just how the Great Rabbis Experiment could have gone wrong. What about those odds I quoted earlier, far greater than a million to one? That's not some tiny little mistake. That's huge! How did it happen?

Remember our dice-throwing experiments in chapter 6? In the first experiment, I tried to cheat by manipulating the dice. I failed. My throws were no better than random.

But in the second test, I didn't try to manipulate the dice. Instead, I just chose carefully which results to report. I rolled three dice at a time. If I saw no sixes, then I didn't record my results. I wound up using about 42 percent of my data.

My results were fabulous — far better than the Great Rabbis Experiment. The data I reported couldn't happen once in a billion billion billion times by random chance. And all I had to do was ignore data I didn't like.

Some scholars have suggested that Witztum, Rips, and Rosenberg somehow ignored some of their own data. The theory goes like this. Suppose you've got a choice between two different spellings for a rabbi's name. Suppose you know that one of those spellings gives a "good" result and the other is rotten. Suppose you'd prefer to see a "good" result. Wouldn't it be easy to find an excellent reason to choose the "good" spelling over the lousy one? Especially if you believed very deeply that you should see "good" results?

That's the danger of wiggle room. You don't need much. Suppose half of your rabbis have unambiguous spellings and the other half have a little wiggle room. You can still get "amazing" results by wiggling the names that you can.

Please bear in mind that Witztum, Rips, and Rosenberg have repeated many times that they did no such thing. I happen to believe that they're honest and honorable men. Even so, the human subconscious is powerful and clever, and our unconscious desires can all too easily influence our actions without our knowing it.

I believe the Great Rabbis Experiment somehow got wiggled. Not much, maybe. Certainly not as much as I wiggled my dice experiment. Then again, their results aren't as amazing as those in my dice experiment. I believe the experiment got wiggled just enough to skew the results.

Don't ask me how, because I don't know. And don't ask for evidence, because I've already given hard evidence in chapters 13 and 14. If I've interpreted my results correctly, then the Great Rabbis Experiment must be incorrect.

But what about other experiments? Recall that Harold Gans followed up the Great Rabbis Experiment with one involving the cities where the rabbis lived. The first version of this Cities Experiment reported highly significant results — the odds were roughly 1 in 200,000. Does this have wiggle room?

Barry Simon's Web site critiques the Cities Experiment. For starters, Simon has performed his own rough version of this experiment. His results are no better than random. Moreover, Simon argues that the philosophy used by Gans "forces wiggle room and it is that wiggle room that allows the result and makes the experiment unrepeatable."

Mr. Gans tells me that, "For the Cities Experiment, I am definitely of the opinion that it has no wiggle room." The spellings of cities were provided by Zvi Inbal, "by application of a very well defined algorithm." Gans is about midway through rechecking in exhaustive detail all spellings used in the Cities Experiment. To date, he's found only a couple of errors. It seems likely that the final result will be close to the original one.

After some reflection, though, I have to agree with Professor Simon. The algorithm created by Inbal is complex, and complexity breeds wiggle room. The calculations I've reported in this book indicate that both the Cities Experiment and Great Rabbis Experiment must have been wiggled — somehow.

But that assumes my own chain of logic is correct, which raises the question...

What If I'm Wrong?

What if I've made a mistake? What if I've got some wiggle room, made a mistake, or just don't understand my own experiments? We'll consider these three questions in turn.

First, is there any wiggle room in my analyses?

No. I don't have to define a strange-looking distance function. I don't have to choose any word-pairs. I don't have to worry about the spellings of names or the encoding of dates.

My entropy analyses look at all digrams and trigrams that actually occur. My chi-squared analyses look at all those expected to occur at least once. If any meaningful information has been encoded, then the frequencies of some of these digrams and trigrams would have been nonrandom. We have seen no evidence of any such meaningful information.

Second, what if I've made a mistake? What if there's some horrible blunder in my math or in my software?

After all the tests I've run, I doubt it. You've seen only the tip of the iceberg in this book. But there's always a possibility that I've made a mistake. I'm not perfect, and my wife can give you plenty of proof of that.

If I've made an error, then somebody's going to find it, because I'm posting the source code for my software on my Web site for public scrutiny. See "A Final Note" at the back of this book for details. If there's a bug somewhere, it'll be found. In that case, I'll post all corrections on my Web site.

Of course, there are mistakes, and then there are MISTAKES.

If somebody tells you that "mistakes have been found in Dr. Ingermanson's work," do yourself a favor. Ask to see the corrected digram and trigram entropy analyses and the corrected digram and trigram chi-squared analyses. If you've read chapters 13 and 14, you'll know how to spot a Bible code. Don't get snookered. Make them show you the evidence. Tiny errors that don't change the results don't count.

Third, what about an error in the interpretation of my results? What if I just haven't understood my own data? What if my results, rightly interpreted, could prove beyond all doubt that the Bible code is real?

In that case we all win. If we prove that the Bible code is real, that will be a huge advance. Right now, most scientists aren't convinced by the Great Rabbis Experiment, because of all that wiggle room. My experiment has no wiggle room. So if my data somehow *proves* the Bible code, then we scientists are going to have to accept that somebody — Somebody — put His signature in the Bible. I could live with that very happily.

But don't hold your breath. I think my results are correct, or I wouldn't put my name on this book.

SPEAKING OF SIGNATURES

Speaking of signatures reminds me that we need to discuss one other author who's written extensively on the Bible code. *The Signature of God* was Grant Jeffrey's first book on the Bible code. He followed it up with *The Handwriting of God* and most recently *The Mysterious Bible Codes*. Jeffrey believes firmly in the authenticity of the Bible code, and his books respond to a number of critics of the code.

Some of these critics have attacked Mr. Jeffrey rather sharply. Much of the criticism looks justified to me, but some of it seems a bit unfair. Furthermore, his latest book presents *new evidence* for a Bible code in the New Testament! That's something we have to look at. It'll only take one more chapter.

THE NOT-SO-MYSTERIOUS BIBLE CODES

In the middle of calculus class one day, my friend Brad suddenly stood up, jabbed a finger at Professor Keith Anderson, and shouted, "Dr. Anderson! YOU'RE WRONG!"

The whole class erupted in laughter. I felt embarrassed for Brad. We'd had a quiz that day, and Brad had missed an important question. He'd spent half the class feverishly flipping through the book, ignoring the lecture. Now he was making a fool of himself. I knew Brad was wrong, because I'd gotten the problem right. I'd done it exactly the way Dr. Anderson had taught us. Brad was being a sore loser, and I wished he'd just sit down and study a little harder next time.

"Sit down, Brad," Dr. Anderson said in a quiet voice. "I don't want to embarrass you publicly by proving right now that you're incorrect. Stop by my office after class, and we'll straighten things out."

That was on a Friday. The next Monday we all sat smirking in our seats waiting for class to begin. Brad slunk in just as the bell rang and sat in the back row. Professor Anderson bounced in after him and stepped to the podium. He looked around the room calmly and then dropped a bombshell. "Brad was correct on Friday," he said. "When I lectured last week on the Chain Rule, I got confused and taught you something incorrect. Thank you, Brad, for setting me straight."

I felt my jaw sag. Brad wasn't exactly the top student in the class. How had he caught the mistake when the rest of us hadn't?

The answer turned out to be simple. Brad hadn't been paying attention in class when Dr. Anderson explained the Chain Rule. So before the quiz, Brad did something novel — he studied the book. I hadn't bothered to do that, because I'd listened during the lectures.

What I learned from this episode goes far beyond calculus. I learned that shouting and derision don't solve arguments. Logic and mutual respect solve arguments. I also learned that everybody makes mistakes, including me.

Grant Jeffrey has written several books covering the Bible code. A number of people have stood up and hollered that Mr. Jeffrey is wrong, *wrong*, WRONG!

There's no need to shout. We're all after the truth, aren't we? So let's discuss this quietly in my office, please.

In this chapter, I'll review Jeffrey's arguments for the Bible code as fairly as I can. You won't be surprised to hear that I often disagree with him, but I'll also point out some cases where he's correct and his critics are wrong. The main reason for spending a whole chapter on Jeffrey is that he has recently announced the discovery of Bible codes *in the New Testament*. We'll analyze this claim using the tools we've developed in this book.

WHAT GRANT JEFFREY SAYS ABOUT THE BIBLE CODE

As of this writing, Grant Jeffrey's latest book is *The Mysterious Bible Codes*. The book expands on the material found in his earlier books, so we'll focus on this latest effort.

Jeffrey's first several chapters will be a review for anyone who's familiar with the Bible code. He discusses some well-known codes, including the Sadat code, the Hitler code, and others; explains the basics of ELSs; gives a brief history of the codes; and then covers the Great Rabbis Experiment.

Next, Jeffrey devotes a full chapter to some cautions about the Bible code. Most Bible-coders agree with him on these, and so do I. The Bible code should not be used to predict the future, Jeffrey says. The code does not reveal any new theology. And it has nothing to do with numerology.

Then Jeffrey covers "new" Bible code discoveries. Some of these, like the death of Princess Diana, are in fact relatively new. Others have been around for quite a while — the AIDS code, the Rabin assassination code, the Gulf War code, the Oklahoma City code, the Toledano kidnapping code, and several more.

Jeffrey spends two chapters covering Yacov Rambsel's work, then a couple of chapters responding to critics.

Then he uncorks a blockbuster announcement. He claims to have found Bible codes in the Greek New Testament! He wraps up the book with an evangelistic appeal.

Are these New Testament codes for real? We'll investigate this question with all due care shortly. First, though, a few words about the earlier parts of his book.

Trivial Errors

I hate to even bring this up, but Jeffrey's book contains an unusual number of minor errors — typos, wrong "facts," and mistaken ideas.

For example, a number of Hebrew words are misspelled, reversed, or transposed. If you read Hebrew, check out pages 11, 27, 72, 83, and 98. Some of these pages have multiple typos.

As another example, Jeffrey gives a howlingly funny (but wrong) explanation of the acronym "Rambam" on page 84. "Robot" indeed! I nearly choked on my Cheerios while reading this at breakfast one morning. "Rambam" is actually a Hebrew acronym for Rabbi Moshe ben Maimon. Jeffrey confused his name with a verse in Exodus that allegedly "encodes" this acronym.

Then on page 50, Jeffrey says that "hidden failures" are a common problem in most scientific research today. This would be big news if it were true, but it isn't. Hidden failures *are* a common problem among astrology buffs, Nostradamus interpreters, and Revelation hype-mongers. And Bible-coders.

There's more, but you get the idea. Jeffrey's book has more errors than

I'm used to seeing in published material. That doesn't discredit his claims, of course. Most books have a few typos (and no doubt mine does too). But along with these low-level examples of careless editing, we find high-level sloppiness in statistics. That *is* a serious problem, and we'll consider it next.

STATISTICAL ERRORS

On pages 33 and 34, Jeffrey mentions a rather well-known code involving the word "Torah." Starting with the last letter of the first word in Genesis, the four Hebrew letters *tav-vav-resh-heh* are found at a skip of 50 letters. Jeffrey quotes Dr. Daniel Michaelson as saying that the odds against this are more than 3 million to 1, based on the letter frequencies in Genesis.

This claim is absurd, apparently a misquote of Michaelson.

First, the naive calculation he describes, using the letter frequencies in Genesis, actually gives odds of 35,148 to 1. That's the obvious part of the mistake.

The second part of the mistake is more subtle. If you've read chapter 5, then you know that this calculation is a postdiction, and you know what can go wrong. In fact, nobody would even bother to look for the word "Torah" at that particular location in Genesis unless they'd already found the first letter *tav*. So an honest probability calculation would compute the probability of finding only the three remaining letters. The odds against finding these letters at a skip of 50 (or at any other skip for that matter) are about 1,870 to 1. But there's nothing magical about a skip of 50. The Bible-coders would be just as happy to find this code at any skip. The odds against finding "Torah" at a skip between 2 and 100 are only about 19 to 1. So the odds of finding this ELS at a reasonably low skip are better than 5 percent! What's so remarkable about that?

It took me less than one minute to do all these calculations using published letter frequencies and a pocket calculator. Why didn't Grant Jeffrey check this wild claim before he quoted it? He should have.

This isn't the only extreme error Jeffrey makes. On page 53, in his discussion of the Great Rabbis Experiment, he says that Witztum, Rips, and Rosenberg calculated the odds of any one of the rabbis' names being so close to the correct birth date, death date, or city of birth. Jeffrey quotes the odds as 1 in 62,500. This is plain wrong. Jeffrey has misread his source. The actual claim made by these researchers was that these were the odds that *the whole set of about 150 word-pairs* would be so closely correlated. Nowhere do they quote odds on a single word-pair for this experiment. In my chapter 16, I've plotted the data from the Great Rabbis Experiment. A number of the word-pairs have a *larger than average distance*. The data is remarkable only because a majority of the word-pairs have a smaller-than-average distance.

Then there's the matter of the alleged Yeshua codes found by Yacov Rambsel. We already discussed the serious problems with Rambsel's work in chapter 15. Jeffrey repeatedly quotes from an article written by Guy Cramer and Lori Eldridge, "Statistical Significance Discovered in the Yeshua Codes," posted on the Prophezine Web site. This article contains a number of naive calculations of postdictions. Like the "3 million to 1" odds for the "Torah" code, such calculations are all too easy to get wrong. Cramer and Eldridge repeatedly made the same mistake. To their credit, they have since repudiated their own article. Grant Jeffrey should too.

On page 137, Jeffrey notes with amazement that some Bible code researchers will consider only ELSs found in an a priori search. (That is, these researchers insist on studying only predictions, not postdictions.) Jeffrey seems not to understand what the scientific method is all about, namely, making predictions and testing them. There's nothing mysterious about the scientific method. And after the investigation we've made in this book, I don't believe there's anything mysterious about the Bible code either.

But Jeffrey Makes Some Good Points

It's rather fun to read chapters 8 and 9 of Grant Jeffrey's book. Here he takes on his critics and catches them in some silliness of their own. They stone his glass house; he stones theirs.

Take the Yeshua codes, for example. As we saw in chapter 15, some

Jewish critics have rightly punched holes in these alleged codes. Yet the Yeshua codes are not substantially different from many other codes that have been claimed — the AIDS codes, the Auschwitz codes, the Garden-of-Eden codes, and dozens of others. Even Jeffrey Satinover's book *Cracking the Bible Code,* which is highly regarded by most Bible-coders, contains many examples of this type of ELS. So why, Jeffrey asks, are these critics attacking him and Rambsel for doing what so many others do?

Good question. Score a point for Jeffrey for detecting hypocrisy. But deduct a point for not realizing that the Yeshua codes are just as ill-founded as the AIDS codes and many others.

Hank Hanegraaff is a Christian who has critiqued Jeffrey sharply in an article entitled "Magic Apologetics," which appeared in the September-October 1997 issue of *Christian Research Journal.* But the example Hanegraaff poses is a gross misrepresentation of the Bible code. Jeffrey quotes this example at length on page 155 and then shreds Hanegraaff's straw-man argument. Jeffrey scores another point for recognizing poor logic.

Jeffrey also answers Hanegraaff's charge that he is using magic apologetics. I think the label is unfair. If the Bible code were real, it *would* be strong scientific evidence that an Author with knowledge of the future dictated the Bible letter for letter. It would be a powerful apologetic to a skeptical generation. But the Bible code isn't real. So there's no point in discussing the apologetic value it *would* have if it *were* real. Sorry, but I can't award a point to either Jeffrey or Hanegraaff here. I think they're both off-base on this one.

NEW TESTAMENT BIBLE CODES?

We still need to consider Jeffrey's claims that he's found a Bible code in the New Testament.

Frankly, I was a little surprised to see this claim in print. Even the best texts of the New Testament show substantially more variation than those of the Hebrew Bible. A good book on this subject is Bruce Metzger's classic,

The Text of the New Testament. If you read Metzger's book, you'll find that the New Testament has been transmitted pretty well, but there are many letter variations, quite a few word variations, and a few suspect passages. Could a real Bible code survive all this?

Jeffrey thinks so. The text he's using is a version of the well-known Textus Receptus (the Greek New Testament Textus Receptus, not to be confused with a Hebrew Bible version of that name which was compiled and printed in the sixteenth century, based on several Masoretic texts). He got this particular version from the German Bible Society. According to Jeffrey's book, you can search for codes in this text on the BibleFind Web site.

I checked out this site, hoping to download the actual Greek text. No such luck. The only thing you can do is search for ELSs online using the BibleFind search engine.

I wanted to test the exact text Jeffrey was using, so I called the folks at BibleFind. The gentleman I spoke with was polite and intelligent. I described my book and explained why I wanted the texts Jeffrey was using. He asked me for a written explanation of my scientific protocols. I didn't have one written yet, and I said so. He pointed out that his group had gone to a lot of effort to get the text from the German Bible Society, and he wasn't free to hand it out to just anyone. I promised to send him a written explanation when I had one ready. He said he'd look forward to seeing it and then we could discuss his texts. He also offered to help me figure out where I'd gone wrong in analyzing the Hebrew texts. I said I'd be happy to publish a correction if he finds a flaw in my work.

The net result is that I struck out. I hope to get the BibleFind texts eventually. If and when I do, I'll analyze them with my software and post the results on my Web site. In the meantime, let's do the best we can with what we've got. In fact, we can do very well, because I have three different versions of the Greek New Testament from other sources.

First we'll examine exactly what Jeffrey reports. Then we'll analyze my Greek texts.

THE Iησου CODE

The most interesting result Jeffrey reports is the discovery of the Greek word Iησου (that is, Jesus) at a number of small skips. Jeffrey searched for all occurrences of this ELS at skips of 22 letters or less. He found 19 different occurrences.

If you know Greek, you may be wondering why Jeffrey chose Iησου, which is the genitive form of Jesus, rather than the more natural Iησους, which is the nominative form. A simple probability calculation suggests the answer.

Based on the letter probabilities of the New Testament, we expect to find Iησου about 24 times at skips of 22 letters or less. We expect to find Iησους only about 2 times. So Jeffrey chose the grammatical form most likely to appear. Nothing wrong with that, although an explanation would have been nice.

What is surprising is that Jeffrey considers his results surprising. We expect 24 occurrences with a spread of about 5. We observe 19 occurrences. That's reasonable. It's not at all remarkable.

Jeffrey finds it significant that most of the 19 occurrences are found in verses that mention Jesus or His teachings. But so what? This *is* the New Testament! The New Testament is rife with verses mentioning Jesus and His teachings. Jeffrey says that these are "important" verses. Here's an experiment you can do. Write down the 19 verses in the New Testament that you consider most important. Now compare them to the ones Jeffrey found. Do you find any overlap? I see only one that *might* make my list.

Jeffrey also goes looking for other codes and finds them — the Greek words for "Blood," "Son," "Innocent," "Lamb," and others. All of his words are five letters or fewer in length, and all contain common Greek letters. It's not surprising that he finds these words. He doesn't do a statistical analysis to measure the significance of his findings.

But we can. We have the tools to measure the statistical significance of all possible "codes" in the New Testament. Let's do that now.

MY SEARCH FOR NEW TESTAMENT CODES

I have three different versions of the Greek text of the New Testament on my computer. One is the Textus Receptus, one is the Byzantine Textform, and one is Nestle's Twenty-Sixth edition. In all likelihood, my version of the Textus Receptus is very close to the one Jeffrey is using but not identical. I expect that any variation between the two will make no difference in the outcome. If anyone thinks otherwise, let him produce the texts and we'll see!

If you've read chapters 13 and 14, you know the drill by now. I'll report the results of digram entropy calculations only since those run most quickly. If we find anything interesting, we'll investigate further. As usual, we'll compute the entropy of 150 random texts and of 150 skip-texts from the originals, then compute Z-scores. We'll set our threshold at a skip of 50.

I ran this test on every book in the Textus Receptus. I also ran it on the first six books in the Byzantine Textform and Nestle's edition. The results are shown below and on the next page in Table 17.1.

Text	Textus Receptus	Byzantine	Nestle's 26th
Matthew	-1.82	-2.02	-4.25
Mark	0.30	-1.73	1.18
Luke	-0.37	0.95	1.89
John	1.07	1.54	3.25
Acts	0.49	-1.02	-0.18
Romans	-0.62	-0.99	-0.62
1 Corinthians	-1.56	–	–
2 Corinthians	2.42	–	–
Galatians	-0.64	–	–
Ephesians	-1.09	–	–
Philippians	-0.57	–	–
Colossians	-2.04	–	–
1 Thessalonians	1.73	–	–
2 Thessalonians	-2.09	–	–

Text	Textus Receptus	Byzantine	Nestle's 26th
1 Timothy	-0.73	–	–
2 Timothy	0.47	–	–
Titus	-1.54	–	–
Philemon	0.16	–	–
Hebrews	-0.68	–	–
James	-0.90	–	–
1 Peter	1.15	–	–
2 Peter	1.29	–	–
1 John	3.12	–	–
2 John	-0.04	–	–
3 John	-1.67	–	–
Jude	-0.93	–	–
Revelation	0.20	–	–

TABLE 17.1: DIGRAM ENTROPY CALCULATIONS FOR THE NEW TESTAMENT

As you can see, only three books show anything interesting, by which I mean a Z-score greater than 3. You may suspect that the "begats" are causing that largish signal in Matthew. There's also some funny business going on in John and 1 John. Could it be that our threshold skip is too low for these books?

The answer is yes. I reran the calculations on the suspicious texts, this time with skips going all the way out to 500. Starting with a threshold of 100, we find the results shown in Table 17.2.

Text	Version	Z-Score
Matthew	Nestle's 26th	-1.29
John	Nestle's 26th	0.99
1 John	Textus Receptus	0.94

TABLE 17.2: SELECTED DIGRAM ENTROPY CALCULATIONS FOR SKIPS UP TO 500

Now we see that the Z-scores are quite normal. In conclusion, we have found no evidence of a Bible code in the New Testament. If you have a different Greek version, you can easily download the software from my Web site and test it yourself. If you find anything remarkable, I'll be glad to post the results on my Web site.

THE BOTTOM LINE

Grant Jeffrey means well in promoting the Bible code so heavily. I just don't believe that he's correct. I don't see any evidence for a Bible code in either the Hebrew Bible or the New Testament.

But on one point I do agree with Jeffrey. In the Bible, I see something far more valuable than a hidden code. We'll discuss that and several other points in the next chapter.

18

PARADIGMS LOST, PARADIGMS FOUND

If you've been awake at all during the last ten years, you've probably heard the buzzword "paradigm shift" tossed around. I must confess that I get a little snippy when I hear this term applied to every trivial new idea that gets fifteen minutes of fame. Historian Thomas S. Kuhn introduced the notion of a paradigm shift in 1962 in *The Structure of Scientific Revolutions*.

Kuhn's book is a good one, although not particularly easy to read. He expects his reader to have some understanding of the history of physics, including Newtonian mechanics, quantum mechanics, and general relativity. I enjoyed the book, mostly because it was the first history book I'd ever read that made more sense to me than to the history students I knew.

In Kuhn's work, a paradigm shift is a revolution in thought, a sudden leap to a new way of looking at the world. A paradigm shift allows the scientist to suddenly view old data from a totally new viewpoint, reinterpreting previous experiments in a radically new way. Real paradigm shifts don't happen very often.

Take Einstein's theory of general relativity, for example. Before Einstein, we had a perfectly good theory of gravitation, developed by Isaac Newton a couple of centuries earlier. In Newton's theory, space was a nice, well-behaved, three-dimensional domain. Time was a concept independent of space. Matter existed in space but had no influence on it. Gravity was a force connecting matter across empty space.

Einstein introduced a radically different view of gravity. No longer do we picture objects acting on each other across flat, empty space. Now we see matter warping space-time and space-time tugging at matter.

That's a paradigm shift.

I'm tempted to say that we've gone through a teensy little paradigm shift in this book. It's nothing like the discovery of general relativity, but we now see the Bible code through a different lens than before. Let's talk about that a bit more.

THE OLD PARADIGM VS. THE NEW

The old paradigm for studying the Bible code was the following: Pick some words and look for them at whatever skips you can find them. Then calculate the probability that you're surprised by what you see.

As we've seen in this book, that paradigm leaves wiggle room, which you can exploit. All you have to do is not report the unsurprising results. If you do find something surprising, then and only then do you report your exciting discovery. We talked about this in chapter 5. You're postdicting when you use this paradigm. Even if you try hard not to postdict, as in the Great Rabbis Experiment, you leave yourself open to accusations of using wiggle room.

Using the old paradigm, you're only going to report the oddball results. Then you'll be tempted to ascribe those results to God or little green men.

The new paradigm used in this book is different. Here, we systematically look at each skip-text as a whole. We examine the digrams and trigrams in that skip-text and check whether the observed frequencies are what we'd expect by random chance.

For small skips, they aren't. We expected that, since natural language has a short-range order (that is to say, redundancy), which we all know about. But that short-range order should have no effect on the skip-texts when we consider large enough skips. As we have seen, if there were a Bible code, the digram and trigram frequencies should not be random at large skips.

We've seen, however, that those frequencies look completely random.

The virtue of the new paradigm is that it squeezes out all the wiggle room. We can't pick and choose the oddball digrams and trigrams. We look at all those that actually occur (in the case of entropy calculations) or all those expected to occur more than once (in the case of the chi-squared calculations).

In the new paradigm we suddenly see the old data in a new way. We see the big picture, not hundreds of handpicked little pictures. The big picture tells us that there is no Bible code. The alleged code is no more meaningful than "nude model Denice" in my scribbles or "Amy" in the alphabet.

For some people, this is good news. My wife, Eunice, told me months before I ran my software that she wanted me to disprove the Bible code. Her reasoning was that she was tired of hearing about people looking for all kinds of weird stuff in the Bible and allegedly finding it. She didn't think God was very happy with that.

So Eunice is glad that I've shown there is no Bible code. But not everyone agrees with her. I can think of two groups of people who are likely to be very unhappy about this: Bible psychics and "codevangelists."

I can't say I feel sorry for those who've been playing Bible Ouija board, predicting the future by looking for ELSs. That's divination, and the Bible forbids it. If you believe the "secret messages" you find encoded in the Bible, then why don't you believe the Bible's plain message that divination is forbidden?

On the other hand, I do have some sympathy for the codevangelists. After all, they mean well. Unfortunately, they're like the movie character Rick, who went to Casablanca "for the waters." He was misinformed. So, too, are the codevangelists, the people who promote the Bible code as a tool for evangelism.

CODEVANGELISTS

The codevangelists fall naturally into three distinct groups: Christians, Messianic Jews, and Orthodox Jews. We'll consider each of these in turn.

A number of Christians have been pursuing the Bible code. A common motivation for this group is apologetics. If the Bible code were proved true, then the Documentary Hypothesis would collapse. We've seen that the Bible code is an illusion. That doesn't prove the Documentary Hypothesis is true, of course. The whole debate just reverts to the status quo, to the pre-Bible-code era. I'm afraid these apologists need to go back to the drawing board; the Bible code is bad apologetics.

Some Messianic Jews have had another motivation for being interested in the Bible code — Yacov Rambsel's alleged "Yeshua codes." These codes have caused quite a bit of friction between Messianic Jews and mainstream Judaism. I've heard rumors of some rather heavy-handed attempts at missionary activities using Rambsel's book. Bad idea. If you're going to try proselytizing Jews, then you'd better have the goods. The Yeshua codes are not the goods.

Orthodox Jews have been the backbone of the Bible-code movement. The best statistical work in support of the Bible code, the Great Rabbis Experiment, came from this milieu. Aish HaTorah (Flame of Torah) is an Orthodox Jewish organization aimed at educating modern Jews about traditional Judaism. One of many topics covered in their Discovery seminar is the Bible code.

I've been to a Discovery seminar. I kept my mouth shut and listened. The presentation was balanced and well done. In the Bible-code talk, the speaker took care to point out the dangers of postdiction. He did not imply that the Bible code has been proven beyond all doubt, nor did he base his arguments for God solely on the Bible code. In my judgment, the Discovery seminar would do just fine if it never mentioned the Bible code again. That's just as well, because I don't think the Bible code is a very good card to play anymore.

WHAT ABOUT YOU?

And what about you? Are you disappointed? Relieved? Confused? Complacent? Angry? Delighted? Now that we've killed the Bible code, where does that leave you?

A Jewish friend of mine happens to know a lot about the New

Testament. Early on in this project, he reminded me of one of the stories Jesus told, the tale of the rich man and Lazarus.

Lazarus, in the story, is a poor, diseased tramp who comes begging at the house of a rich man. Unable to get food or healing, Lazarus dies and is taken to the bosom of Abraham. The rich man also dies, but he goes to Hades. Seeing Lazarus and Abraham at a distance, he begs for relief from his misery, but Abraham explains he cannot be helped. The rich man then asks Abraham to send Lazarus back to warn his five brothers. Abraham replies that the brothers have the Torah and the Prophets. If they pay no attention to those witnesses, then they will not be convinced to repent even by someone returning from the dead.

My friend and I drew the following application from this story. If you're not interested in reading the plain text of the Bible, then what earthly good could a Bible code do you?

Fact is, I think there are excellent reasons to believe in God and powerful reasons to love and revere the Bible. To discuss these fully would require another book. Maybe I'll write that book someday.

In the meantime, if you want a message from God, consider this. The Bible is a rich, complex, and powerful book with many layers of meaning. The real secrets of the Bible are "hidden in plain sight."

Go get 'em!

The Bible code is dead. Long live the Bible!

19

A Final Note: About the Math and the Software

My software for studying the Bible code will be posted on my Web site on the publication date of this book:

http://www.rsingermanson.com

You don't need any special technical skills to get this, other than the ability to drive a Web browser and install software on your computer.

Also at this Web site you'll find articles that serve as "appendices" for this book:

Appendix A: Statistics
Appendix B: Chi-squared Analyses
Appendix C: Entropy
Appendix D: Technical Notes on Digrams and Trigrams

These four articles are intended for technical readers who would like to verify the correctness of the results reported in this book. (My intent is that the main ideas of the book should be understandable without reading these appendices.) The math to be presented in these articles should make sense to someone with an undergraduate degree in math, science, engineering, or related disciplines.

Web sites are notoriously ephemeral. I won't guarantee that this site will be there a hundred years from now, but I'll keep it going at least as long as this book is in print. You'll find a set of Java programs there that will allow you to reproduce the results I've shown in this book.

For technical readers, I'll also post the source code for my programs, so you can verify that my software actually computes what it's supposed to compute.

I think that buying this book entitles you to something. Therefore, the first release of the software will be free, although it will *not* be public domain. Basically that means you can use it, modify it, or give it away, but you can't sell it. Eventually I may produce a fancier commercial version with a nicer user interface and more bells and whistles.

Enjoy it now while it's free!

NOTE ADDED IN PROOF

During the typesetting of this book, there have been some new developments around the world, regarding the Bible code:

1. Several prominent code-meisters will shortly publish an important article that complements my case. As of today, I'm sworn to secrecy—I can't even tell my editor. However, by the time you read these words, the article will be in print, and I'll have posted an analysis on my Web site.

2. Chuck Missler recently published his book *Cosmic Codes,* trying to put the Bible code in a broader context. I don't buy his ideas, but the book is worth reading. See the review of his book on my Web site.

3. Harold Gans has released a preliminary result on his new and improved Cities Experiment. He quotes odds of six in a million and tells me this experiment has no wiggle room. Doron Witztum has also run some new experiments claiming no wiggle room. I'm skeptical but open. I look forward to seeing complete write-ups on these experiments.

I've shown in this book that any skip-text of Genesis has far fewer than 700 letters encoded. This kills the usual notion of a Bible code, in which encoded ELSs run rampant. However, a believer can postulate a "sparse Bible code" with a few real codes hidden like golden needles in a vast haystack. My work does not *absolutely* disprove this idea. (What if God encoded exactly one word? My tests would miss it.) So Gans and Witztum could *conceivably* be right. But what principle allows them to find so many needles in a haystack so poor in metal? Can they predict where to find new needles?

4. Recently I have sharpened my calculations. I have now proven that *far fewer than 200 characters in any skip-text of Genesis are encoded.* Details are on my Web site. For those who see needles in that haystack, show me the metal!